the NO-NO LIST

How to Spot Mr. Wrong
So You Can Find Mr. Right

Venus Rouhani, MA

Licensed Marriage and Family Therapist

RIVER GROVE
BOOKS

Published by River Grove Books
Austin, TX
www.rivergrovebooks.com

Distributed by River Grove Books

Design and composition by Greenleaf Book Group and Sheila Parr
Cover design by Greenleaf Book Group and Sheila Parr
Cover images: ©Shutterstock/schab; ©Shutterstock/Alexander Ryabintsev; ©Shutterstock/ phipatbig

Cataloging-in-Publication data is available.

Print ISBN: 978-1-63299-058-7

eBook ISBN: 978-1-63299-059-4

First Edition

To my husband, Faraj, of more than four decades, whose love and relationship provided the material and concept for this book.

And to my father, Amir, who gave me the foundation of critical thinking and the yearning for finding solutions to problems surrounding us.

Contents

Chapter 1

X X X ✓

The Wrong Question: What Do I Want?

What Keeps Going Wrong?

When it comes to dating, do you feel as if you are doing all the right things but still picking all the wrong people? You have been told, "Just be yourself, look for someone who shares your interests and values, and you will find the right mate for you." But you have fallen in love before, maybe more than once, and you were shocked to find that someone who once made you so happy could go on to make you so miserable. Not only did they hurt or infuriate you, but they also made you feel bad about yourself. The person you fell for was not as advertised. By the time you learned the ugly truth, you had invested so much in the relationship that you still tried to hold on to the dream. Eventually the issues grew too big to bear and one or both of you decided to give up.

Now you are dating again, wondering whether lasting love even exists and whether you should ever trust your emotions. The answer is: yes and no.

Yes, there is such a thing as lasting love,
but trusting your emotions exclusively
is probably not the best way to go.

I am not claiming that chemistry is unimportant. You need that initial spark to get things started, but you also need to understand that such a spark is not sufficient to keep things going. The truth is, if you are picking your dates the way most people do—solely looking for chemistry and what you have in common—you are doing it wrong. Don't feel bad. Even rational people do it wrong. In fact, even people who wind up with great relationships often get there by chance.

There *is* a better way.

First, let's look at the potential results of doing it wrong. It starts with asking the wrong question: What do I want? Someone funny? Smart? Attractive? Athletic? Talented? Independent? That's what Cindy and Jeff asked themselves, and look what happened to them:

What Cindy and Jeff Did Not Know

Cindy was a beautiful forty-eight-year-old woman. She had been married for a couple of years in her twenties. After that marriage ended in divorce, she dated quite a bit, but for more than twenty years she could not make any of her relationships last. By the time she turned forty-two, she was a single successful artist, working three days a week and generating a handsome six-figure income.

That is when Cindy met Jeff, a financial analyst four years her senior. Jeff had recently divorced his wife of sixteen years, had two adult children, and held a corporate job that also paid a generous six figures. That is, until the economy tanked in 2009 and he lost his job. Subsequently, he had to take a job as a book-keeper, and began making only a third of his previous income. That didn't bother Cindy.

Cindy was the kind of woman Jeff thought he wanted: beautiful and talented with an independent spirit. Similarly, Jeff was the kind of man Cindy thought she wanted: attractive and charming with a respectable job. They shared mutual interests, such as traveling, hosting parties, and going out.

Cindy and Jeff had been in and out of their relationship for six years when they decided to seek couples therapy with me. The following are a few things we unearthed during their sessions. As you read, note that the traits that originally attracted these partners turned out to hide unexpected issues:

What Cindy and Jeff Learned the Hard Way

1. Cindy at first liked the fact that Jeff enjoyed going out and having fun. The problem was, he didn't party in moderation. In fact, he was a high-functioning alcoholic. Cindy said that on weekends his drinking got out of hand and sometimes he had blackouts.

2. Jeff was very flirtatious with women. Although his flirtation was what first attracted Cindy to him, such ongoing behavior toward other women, especially his coworkers, bothered her. His behavior encouraged coworkers to call and text him at all times of the day and night. His excuse was that these women were "just friends" and that he wanted to "be there" for his friends when they needed him.

3. Jeff was a friendly guy who put himself out there for other people, which Cindy liked. But he carried it too far for Cindy's taste by remaining in close contact with his ex-wife. He answered his ex's calls and texts at all hours, even when he and Cindy were on a date or a trip together.

4. Although Jeff enjoyed the lifestyle that Cindy's income made possible—dinner dates, parties, and travel—he resented that Cindy made three times as much money as he did despite working fewer hours. He was vocal about what he considered an unfair job market that valued her talent over his education. "She makes so much, working only three days a week, as an *artist*?" he said in a demeaning voice. What's more, he directly told Cindy that she had merely gotten lucky, discounting the validity of both her talent and her independent profession.

5. Jeff loved Cindy's free spirit, but her independence did not allow him as much control of the relationship as he felt he needed.

All the signs of these character and personality differences had been present early on. But both Jeff and Cindy had intentionally muted or downplayed them in hopes that the other person would change. Through therapy, they came to realize they were not a healthy match and decided to split. Wouldn't it have been better if they had been able to see this ahead of time, rather than wasting six years of their lives and emotions on the wrong person?

How could they have known?

Here's how: by asking the right question. The wrong question is, "What do I want?" The right question is: "What *don't* I want?"

Having Things in Common Is Simply Not Enough

American culture cultivates an emphasis on knowing what we want. Among modern adults, the question, "What do I want?" seems to come up most often when seeking a mate. But how can you know what you want in a suitable life partner if you have never had one before?

It is easy to know what you fantasize. Maybe you want someone with fair hair, an athletic body, and kind eyes. Or perhaps someone educated and romantic who makes you laugh. Or maybe it is your hope that lightning will strike: you will meet Mr. or Ms. Right and love will arrive to solve all your problems. We know that is not effective. If it were, nobody who fell in love and married would ever divorce.

Experts estimate between 30 and 41 percent of marriages end in divorce. Clearly, Americans can use better criteria to find a mate.

Modern psychology suggests that it *is* important to share common interests and values with a potential partner. However, the many couples I have encountered, both personally and professionally, have led me to conclude that using the "we have so much in common" barometer alone is a terrible way to measure a couple's potential success. Let's say you like hiking, movies, cooking, and dogs. You can easily meet hundreds of people who like those things too. Let's say on top of that you also prefer someone who shares your political and spiritual views, makes family a priority, and believes in pursuing a career with a purpose. You can walk into almost any social gathering of your peers and meet someone like that, especially since most people gravitate toward groups with similar values and interests. That is how most people look for dates. But are most of the people you know having success at it?

Looking for someone with common interests and values is very popular. But it does not work.

Why is having things in common not enough? Because the same man who loves dogs, children, and long walks on the beach may also have a temper, or wandering eyes, or a drinking problem. Because the woman who loves tennis, travel, and dressing up for Comic Con may also be needy, or controlling, or a workaholic.

World-renowned psychologist Dr. John Gottman, known for his research on marital stability, has found that only 31 percent of the issues between marital partners are resolvable (*The Marriage Clinic*, John Gottman, Norton Professional Books). I believe that this 31 percent represents the areas of life in which partners share interests and values in common, the characteristics couples initially look for. It's important to consider the flip side of that number. According to Gottman, 69 percent of the issues that life partners face are *irresolvable*. In my opinion, these irresolvable issues are based on individual differences in personalities and needs. Some of these differences are non-negotiable: things we simply cannot tolerate in another person.

I like to visualize this juxtaposition of what couples share in common and what they don't as two overlapping rings. If you take two wedding rings and turn them into a Venn diagram that represents the reality of relationships, they might look something like this:

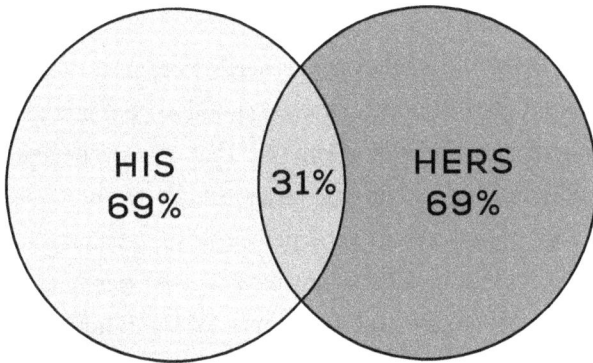

Figure 1.1

The place where the wedding bands overlap represents the 31 percent of their lives that couples share in common, while the place where the bands lie separate and alone represents the other 69 percent of their lives that couples don't share in common.

The thing all couples need to understand is that even when we have plenty in common with our partners, mostly we don't. Still, even though many of the personality and character differences between people are not negotiable, the problems they cause are conquerable. The solution I offer to people who are looking for a mate is to prepare their list of non-negotiables *before* they choose a partner. I call it the **No-No List**.

The trick is figuring out ahead of time whether those things you do *not* have in common are things you can live with. This is critical because you cannot change another person, nor should you want to. Plenty of research shows that when people lead lives that deviate from their true natures and capabilities, they are less likely to be happy than those individuals whose goals are in sync with the way they want to live their lives. If you try to change another person, you are telling that person that he or she is somehow defective or not good enough. That puts you on unequal ground, and that is a bad place for a relationship to stand.

Each person in a relationship needs to respect the partner's 69 percent, even if that means saying goodbye, because those are the things that make each of you *you*. That 69 percent represents your individuality, something relationships are not meant to destroy, but to preserve. That 69 percent is so resistant to change because it represents your character and your personality, your experiences of the past and your hopes for the future, the values you have been taught and those you have developed on your own. So when someone tries to change this part of you, *of course* it causes resentment. It translates into, "I only love the part of you I shopped for. I don't love all of you." Nobody wants that.

People who try to change their partner's 69 percent, that outer ring of individuality, end up in unhappy marriages or relationships. Those are the married clients I see who feel stuck, confined, or imprisoned. Seeing that happen is what causes so many single people to say they don't want to get married, because "If I get married, I'll have to change myself." No wonder so many people see marriage as a sort of death. If you had to change to make yourself 100 percent suitable to another person, it would indeed be the death of the majority of yourself. Over time, if you cannot accept the other person as is, it will create resentment in both of you. You will resent your partner for not changing, and your partner will resent you for trying to force that change.

A client I know runs a social networking club. He is an extrovert and loves to be around people. When he chose a wife, he chose someone with whom the areas inside their overlap were strong, and whose areas outside that overlap were things he could live with. Still, they both had to come to terms with accepting one non-negotiable item: he loves the social aspect of his business that sometimes requires him to be out late partying, but his wife sometimes loves to be cozy at home in the evenings and go to bed by ten.

Neither of them is right or wrong in this matter; she's not a party-pooper because she won't go out with him all the time, and he's not inconsiderate because he leaves her alone sometimes. She likes their home. He likes hanging out with friends and clients. What's more, in so many other ways they are compatible, and even in many of the areas where they aren't compatible they do support each other. There was just this one no-no for both of them. They decided it was worth it to compromise, so before they married they came to an agreement.

She more-or-less said, "I'll go out with you sometimes to keep you company, but when I'm tired don't push me. In return, I'll trust you to spend time on your own without me and to enjoy the opportunity to be alone."

He said, "I'll accept that you can't go out with me every night, so long as I can still go without worrying about you feeling neglected. I understand that sometimes you need to just crawl in bed and read a book. Meanwhile, I don't have to go out every night. Some nights, I'll be happy to curl up with you."

That works for them. Other people might find that an untenable situation. They would feel worried about leading separate lives. For such people, these items might go on their **No-No List** as big negatives: "Homebody" versus "Parties all the Time."

It can take years in any relationship to realize that some of the 69 percent of things you do not hold in common actually matter, even if you told yourself in the beginning that they did not matter at all. Then you will face a tough decision. Some people decide it is worth it to stick together, but many just cannot go on. It is hard to blame them. If your spouse is a little sloppy, that's one thing, but a hoarder is something else entirely. It is better to ask *beforehand*, "Is this the wrong person to marry?" rather than to ask *afterward*, "Do I need a divorce?"

Chapter 2

X X X ✔

Changing the
Myths About Marriage

Falling in Love First and Asking Questions Later

No matter how much you have in common with a romantic partner, the math remains the same: the largest portion of the relationship will always fall *outside* the area that you and your partner share in common. At the end of the day, you are still individuals. All those interests and values you have in common will never hold you together if the negatives that lie outside that common area include things you can never accept. So, since marital issues will rarely originate from the areas you and a partner have in common, and since most of the relationship will fall outside that area, you need to change the questions you're asking—before you even think about getting married.

Why do people spend so much time asking,
"What *do* we have in common?" and so
little time asking, "What *don't* we have in
common, and can I live with that?"

Many people make the mistaken assumption that finding love is only an act of seeking, not avoiding. They assume that if they find what they seek, there is no point looking for problems with what they have found. They believe the relationship problems they have had in the past were unavoidable because their previous partners either consciously or unconsciously hid their negative traits at the start. But I have discovered that people typically reveal themselves early on, if only we pay attention. Often we are so eager to fall in love that we engage in wishful thinking. We fail to notice red flags, or kid ourselves that they're no big deal, or chide ourselves for being judgmental, or tell ourselves that nobody's perfect. The fear of ending up alone can prompt us to see only what we want to see.

A leap of faith is romantic and worth taking. But looking before you leap can help you ensure that the romance stays alive in the long term. Sadly, when people come to me for counseling, it is often already too late. They have picked the wrong partner and there is not much they can do to change that. But they have invested months or years in the relationship and they hate to feel they have wasted their time. So they tell themselves that therapy will change the other person, or maybe even help them change themselves. But most of these problems spring from deeply embedded character traits, values, and ideals that define who people are. There are only two ways to go at that point: either you come to terms with the thing you thought you could not stand and stop making yourself and your partner crazy by trying to change it, or you break it off.

After seeing the pain people go through in making these choices, it has occurred to me over and over again: Wouldn't it be better if we could make these choices *before* we invest ourselves in another person?

What Shelly and Matt Did Not Know

Consider Shelly and Matt, a couple who met when they were both going through their medical residency. They had a lot in common: they were two doctors who admired each other's intelligence and tenacity, who shared similar ambitions and understood each other's tough schedules, and who made each other laugh. They hit it off right away, dated for two years, and got married. During their residency, Shelly had noticed that the nurses and hospital staff often hit on her handsome young husband. So when Shelly went into private practice while Matt remained based at a hospital, Shelly grew nervous. She wanted to be in touch with Matt at all times and would grow jealous if he did not return her calls right away. She called more and more frequently, often showing up at the hospital unannounced to check up on Matt. She eventually started to check his phone and emails.

At first Shelly was proud that other women found her man attractive, but over time she grew increasingly paranoid and jealous. At first Matt saw Shelly's constant calls and appearances as evidence of her love for him, but over time he felt she was pulling him away from his social and professional life and trying to control his every move. He felt suffocated. She felt ignored. After sixteen years and two children, they divorced.

It did not have to be that way: Shelly knew from the start what her husband's social and professional life was like, and Matt knew from the start that Shelly needed constant reassurance and attention. But each of them dismissed the red flags and what those might mean for the future. If they had made a **No-No List** before they started dating anyone, they would have asked themselves what kind of issues would be a deal breaker in a relationship. With that list, they could have been on their way to connecting the dots and seeing where they were likely to end up—before they even started.

I remember a client who told me that her husband of fourteen years had developed a temper. She swore he did not have a short fuse at the beginning of their relationship, that it had only started a couple of years before. Then I asked what he was like when they were dating. She said he was sweet and romantic. He used to take her out to dinner. "He was a good tipper," she said. *Hmmm, what does that have to do with this?* Then she turned on the light bulb: "Unless they really screwed it up. Oh my God, if the waitress didn't bring the right thing, he would lose it. He'd make a scene and he wouldn't leave a tip at all." She said that was the *only thing* that had bothered her when they were dating. Except it wasn't. He also had road rage, sometimes actually chasing drivers who cut him off. She saw these as isolated incidents, but they were red flags. "This guy always had a temper," I told her.

Why didn't she see it? Because early in the relationship he was not aiming his temper at *her.* If she had ever bothered to make a **No-No List**, she might have written "Foul Temper" at the top of her list. Then she might have thought twice before going on another date with him.

Many people assume that all the things they have in common will help them get through anything together. So they find someone who attracts them, check to make sure they "have plenty in common," and then they invest a lot of time, energy, and emotion into making the rest of it work. They ignore red flags early on because those flags do not pertain to the question: what do we have in common? By the time they see the flags for what they are, it is too late. They feel as if they have been blindsided. Soon they are living in a siege of "why do you do this?" and "why don't you ever do that?" until they either have to end a bad relationship, or rationalize hanging on to it. Love alone will not be enough to save the relationship.

Most premarital compatibility tests and premarital counseling programs are designed primarily to identify what couples have in common. In any partnership, if you want it to be successful, then compatibility is crucial. However, long-term compatibility is not just a matter of having things in common. That's the easy part. It is also a matter of understanding how strongly those things we *don't* have in common will affect our partnership. That's one reason so many employers ask people to identify their weaknesses as well as their strengths during a job interview. This process of deciding whom to date is ultimately more important than a job interview, as it could lead to a partnership that you hope to keep for the rest of your life.

Existing premarital tests and programs barely touch upon a couple's ability to negotiate what they *don't* have in common or what they cannot tolerate. To fill this gap, I go into more detail with couples during our premarital/pre-relationship sessions. Sometimes I feel a wall of resistance going up and have to separate the couple to get them to even admit that they disagree at times. This wall might not be obvious to an untrained observer. The wall is built on the belief that nothing can go wrong because "we're in love." But real love has been tested by real problems. I see warning signs whenever couples seem just too perfect: holding hands too much, extolling each other's virtues too much, and defending each other too much.

Once I separate the couples for individual sessions, I often find many items that are liable to cause problems down the road. Typically they have never negotiated these differences before and probably never would have if they had not come to counseling.

When I point these issues out, most of them declare that they will work it out because they love each other.

It is essential to understand that love alone cannot resolve non-negotiable differences.

The Best Matchmaking Works Backward

I take a different, some might say backward, approach to advising people on selecting a mate. Over the years, many friends and acquaintances, perhaps influenced by my strong marriage and reliable personal advice, have asked me to introduce them to potential mates. These same individuals remain happily married. When I became a counselor, I began deconstructing my matchmaking method to see if I could figure out why it worked.

It turned out that I never started by asking people to tell me about themselves, or to tell me what they wanted in another person, or what kind of common interests were important to them. Instead, since most of them were friends, I would say something like, "I already know so much about you. So tell me, what is it you *don't* like in a man (or woman)? What is it you *don't* want in a relationship?" With someone I did not know well, I would ask both what that person was looking for *and* what he or she wanted to stay away from. Even though I am a positive person by nature, my biggest focus was always on the negatives they described. I was asking them for a **No-No List**.

Some would say things like, "I hate someone who's irresponsible" or "I can't handle someone who's controlling." That was when I asked probing questions and took notes. When people tell you what they *like*, it is usually pretty straightforward, but when people share what they *don't* like, it can be very revealing.

The reason we hate certain things has to do with deep aspects of our character and/or pivotal events in our personal history. These become non-negotiables, what I call No-Nos.

There is a reason we hate some negatives more than others. In theory, *nobody* would like someone irresponsible, stingy, or controlling, yet those words are hot buttons for some individuals and not others. Think about it: one woman sees "irresponsible" where another sees "carefree," one man sees "controlling" where another sees "strong." When the word "controlling" pops up on someone's **No-No List,** it tells me much more about the person using the term than merely the kind of people he or she wants to avoid. It may signal that this person is highly independent, or had few opportunities to make decisions while growing up, or suffered a past trauma of being forced to do something, or any number of other possibilities.

The most difficult task to ask a counseling client to perform is: "Define yourself." If I ask clients, "Tell me something about yourself," they often give me lists of roles they play, things they do, labels they live by. "I'm a mother. I'm an accountant. I like to ski. I have a large family and I'm the youngest." They are often unfamiliar with their internal life, the things that drive them to take on those roles.

How can you know what kind of a mate you want if you do not know who you are? I have discovered that by asking people, "What *don't* you like?" they begin to answer the question, "Who are you, really?" When someone answers by saying, "It irks me when people don't take responsibility for their actions," I immediately know that the person saying this is a very responsible person. To learn more about what makes this person tick, my next questions might be, "Why? Can you give me an example? How do you feel when that happens?" This exploration gives me a clearer picture of the person. Even if we do not go much beyond "I hate irresponsible people," I can begin to help this individual pick the right mate, because it is clear: This is someone who will never be able to live with a mate who pushes that button.

Marriage Theories Need an Update

Today you often hear young people declaring they hate relationships or do not believe in marriage. Some call it a trap. Some see marriage as a death of the individual. I believe that is partly because the popular psychology that evolved from the 1960s and '70s has taught us to emphasize independence and self-actualization, while marriage theories are still stuck in the '40s and '50s with that era's ideas of surrender and sacrifice. It makes sense to me that people born since the '70s are afraid that if they get married their individuality will disappear. When they do get married, their psyches get caught in a tug-of-war: Am I taking care of myself or being selfish? Am I helping my mate or being codependent? As each partner struggles with these contradictions, resentment builds: "You won't let me be myself!" versus "All you think about is yourself!"

We need a new vision of marriage that bridges this gap between independence and interdependence.

From the 1930s to the 1950s, when people married they gave up all their personal needs and wants for the greater good of the family. Women were expected to give up their interests outside the domestic sphere, and men were expected to give up their aspirations outside being a provider. Then, from the '60s to the '90s, we began to judge the quality of our lives by different standards. We learned that happiness could factor in personal fulfillment. This could run the gamut from "If it feels good, do it!" to "Find your purpose." Instead of it being all about "us," it was all about "me." I believe that if we can bridge that gap, modern marriage could become something more powerful than ever.

Today, marriage is an opportunity to find fulfillment both in contributing to the greater good of the family and in leveraging the support of our partners to help us fulfill our individual needs, goals, and dreams. In modern marriage, we seek a blend of give and take, sacrifice and support, togetherness and independence, what we can build together and what we can build when apart. We can enjoy a certain amount of interdependence without becoming codependent, and we can enjoy a certain amount of independence without becoming selfish.

The **No-No List** will tell you about those aspects of potential partners that are liable to become sources of their independence, the part of their life that will be separate from yours. It will also tell you about those aspects of potential partners that might make them less likely to accept your individuality.

It is important to take care of yourself first, so that you feed your energy and spirit to take care of others, which in turn makes you feel personally fulfilled. The modern ideal in relationships is to combine individuality with mutual respect. No marriage is easy or perfect, but a couple can survive hard times by each coming to respect the part of the other's life that is not in his or her control. This is easiest if you choose your partner well in the first place. That means seeking someone with whom you can come to terms on the 69 percent of that person's values, behaviors, and interests that you do not share in common—the non-negotiables. This way, your **No-No List** will not become the hidden deal breaker in your long-term relationship.

Chapter 3

X X X ✓

Why You Need a List

When Chemistry Explodes

It is human nature to seek chemistry in romance, and I agree that an initial attraction is important. But if you are only looking for points of connection, then 69 percent of you is in trouble, because 69 percent of your life will always function independently of your romantic partner—no matter how great the chemistry is. The problem is that the 31 percent of your life where your chemistry connects with someone else's is pretty powerful, so powerful that it can make you forget logic and reason. That kind of dependence on chemistry is what blows up relationships. If you want a loving relationship that will not threaten to explode on you in the long term, you are going to have to figure out how to bring your rational brain into the picture.

Different areas of the brain function in different ways. For our purposes, allow me to give you a quick look at two areas of the brain:

The Brain You Need to Know
1. **Cerebrum:** This part of your brain, specifically the left cerebrum, controls judgment, reasoning, and logic.

2. **Amygdala:** The amygdala is part of the limbic system. The limbic system controls emotions, instincts, and short-term emotional memories. The amygdala deals with the fight-or-flight response, the avoidance of pain and danger, and the pursuit of pleasure and survival. Your amygdala decides many things before your cerebrum or rational brain kicks in, such as:

   • I feel safe vs. I don't feel safe
   • I like this person vs. I hate this person
   • I could mate with this person vs. "Not on your life!"

When the amygdala hijacks our thought processes, all reasoning goes out the door. That is precisely what we need to prevent by using the reasoning cerebrum to plan ahead for those moments. Your **No-No List** will help you work with your amygdala, instead of letting it completely take over.

When people have been through trauma in past relationships, with anyone from their parents to their ex-lovers or ex-spouses, their amygdala tends to work on overdrive. That is one important reason to find out what your negative triggers are beforehand. You are never going to stop your amygdala from reacting, but what you can do is bring reason to your reactions. That is the job of your left cerebrum, the boss of your rational brain. If you know what your no-no triggers are ahead of time, your left cerebrum can rationally figure out which ones you can work with and which ones you can't. So when the time comes, you will be better prepared to tell the difference between Mr./Ms. Right and Mr./Ms. Wrong.

Creating and learning your **No-No List** is a little bit like planning and practicing a fire drill. You keep doing the fire drill over and over until it seems silly and pointless. Then when there is a real fire and your fight-or-flight response kicks in, your rational brain can tell your primal brain: "Wait, I have the plan for our survival!" The amygdala, which wants you to survive, will then let the cerebrum take you to safety.

If a woman has drilled herself on her **No-No List**, then when her amygdala notices a hot, funny, smart man and says, "This one makes me want to reproduce ASAP!" the cerebrum shouts, "Not so fast! I have a plan for our long-term survival, called the **No-No List**, and it says we don't want a man who talks about himself all the time. He might be too self-centered to help take care of that baby you want to make."

Meanwhile, a man's amygdala might notice a woman who is hot, funny, and smart, but his cerebrum warns him, "Sure, she's cute, but she's making me feel unsafe by acting needy! My **No-No List** says we don't want a clingy woman who is too dependent. The go-getter across the room might contribute more to our long-term survival."

Once you know your No-No List, your primitive amygdala will still cue you to chemistry, but your rational cerebrum will evaluate each prospect in terms of long-term partnership.

If you were picking a partner for your business, you would not just consider whether a potential candidate looked good, or made you laugh, or offered you excitement. Those things might come into play, but if you wanted the business to last you would also consider the candidate's background: What skills and talents does this candidate bring to the table? What kind of work ethic does this candidate have? Does this candidate play well with others? You would especially want to know if he or she has some character flaw that you cannot stand. Does this one seem prone to exaggeration, indicating boasting or dishonesty? Does that one blame other people when problems arise, indicating a victim mentality or a resistance to teamwork?

Part of you might resist thinking of love in terms of a business partnership, but at the end of the day a marriage or any long-term relationship can definitely have that component. Marriage is a long-term partnership that combines not only lives, but also incomes, property, assets, and all of the goals and dreams that go with that. If you are not ready to look at things in those terms, then you are letting your primitive side do your rational thinking for you. If you do that, you are liable to find out the hard way just how much of a business transaction love can become—when you have to split everything in a divorce or breakup.

Throughout childhood, you connected in very instinctive and emotional ways with your family. The experiences you had during that time continue to shape many of your most instinctive reactions throughout your life. Whether your primary family made you feel safe or frightened or some combination of the two, the effects have left you with a host of buttons you do not want pushed, and the brain quickly accesses those buttons during charged situations.

Those knee-jerk instincts are why police officers receive plenty of training on how to interact with people at a crime scene, because crime scenes are full of triggers that can set off people's deepest fears and anxieties. The cops learn their own **No-No Lists**, or protocols, with the goal of giving the officers a way to rationally disengage from emotional triggers so they can focus on the professional jobs they are there to do. This requires training and practice.

> Relationship conflicts can be as full of
> emotional triggers as crime scenes. Like
> police, we can all use training and practice
> to prepare for crises before they arise.

In relationships, it is useful to have protocols to help us disengage from automatic responses so we can focus on the things we want from our loved ones: companionship, partnership, friendship, sex, love, children, family, home, and more. We cannot have all of those things if we are spending 69 percent of our time struggling with emotional buttons that keep getting pushed. If you have ever spent most of a relationship trying to shut off those buttons, it may be because you never stopped to rationally plan the protocols that would prevent a lot of that button pushing. What's more, perhaps you never established the boundaries that might have prevented you from ending up in such a painful partnership in the first place.

The Shopping Trip of a Lifetime

I am not saying that you should ignore people who excite you. Your amygdala knows a thing or two about survival, or humans would not have lasted this long. If someone catches your eye with a smile, catches your ear with a great story, or catches your heart by discovering an interest or philosophy that both of you share, then pay attention. Just make sure you are armed with information about yourself that will help you pay attention to *everything*, not only the things that instantly please or frighten you. The information you need to pay special mind to should be on your **No-No List**. That list will tell you whether or not all those things that grab your attention might also come with some deal breakers you want nothing to do with. With your **No-No List**, your rational self and your reactive self can work together to give you better results.

Let me give you another way to think of the **No-No List**. Sometimes when you go clothes shopping you make an impulse purchase, while other times you know more about what you want. Have you noticed that the impulse purchases are the ones most likely to end up gathering dust in the closet? That may be because you forgot to consider whether you had any shoes or pants to go with that cute accessory, or you hoped you would lose weight to fit into it but you didn't, or you loved it so much you ignored the fact that it is not a good color on you. Have you noticed that the clothes you wear most are the ones you picked when you had a clear idea of what you wanted and why?

I believe you are even more likely to find just the right thing when you also know what you *don't* want, and why.

Say you need a new dress for a party with your coworkers. You might figure you will know what you like when you see it. However, you can easily list a few things you know you do not want.

A Sample No-No List for Dress Shopping:

1. Nothing too short or too low-cut because it might send the wrong message to male coworkers
2. Nothing too businesslike either, because this is a party and a chance to show off your lighter side
3. Nothing black, because you already have two little black dresses in your closet and why buy something you already have?

4. Nothing too dressy because you are going to someone's house and you want to feel and project relaxation

5. Nothing too casual either, because you want to show that you respect yourself and others enough to be at your best

6. Nothing more than $100 because you are on a budget

7. Nothing that requires you to buy new shoes because you have too many shoes already

8. Nothing pastel, green, orange, or striped because experience has told you those do not flatter you

9. Nothing lacy or frilly or pink because you do not want to project a stereotypical image of submissive femininity in a roomful of powerful men

10. Nothing from that one department store, because last time you went there somebody else showed up in the same dress.

With the above list, you are at the magic number 10, which is what I also suggest for a working **No-No List** for romance. It is easy to learn and remember, so there is no need to carry it around if you don't want to. If you look more closely at the list, you will realize it also tells you something about the woman who made it: she knows herself, at least when it comes to clothes. Even though it is full of no-nos, it is the kind of list that makes it easier for this woman to recognize just what will constitute a *yes-yes*. The chemistry still has to be there, but she will bypass a lot of searching through clothes with chemistry that might call to her but that would be all wrong for her needs. She is more likely to find the perfect dress in no time, and more likely to feel confident at the party.

It works more or less the same way with a car. You might buy a car impulsively. You might think, "This sports car is a chick-magnet, the horsepower under the hood is exciting, the red color shouts confidence." Then you drive it home only to realize that it gets lousy gas mileage, that you paid extra to go from zero-to-sixty in a few seconds even though you live in a city with so much stop-and-go traffic that such a feature is useless to you, and that red cars get more speeding tickets. A wise car buyer would plan ahead, not only keeping a lookout for the features that attract him, but also for the ones he needs to avoid, such as: (1) Nothing that gets below 25 miles per gallon, (2) nothing that costs more than $25,000, (3) nothing red, and so on.

If you buy a car with drawbacks, you probably figure, "I bought it, so I'm stuck with it." You do not want to end up saying that after you pick a mate with drawbacks.

Many people treat marrying the wrong person like buying the wrong car: "I signed the contract. It's not all bad. It would be too much trouble to take it back. I guess I have to live with it." In marriage, it gets more complicated, but you can see the similarity in thinking: "I made a commitment. I still love her. I don't want to go through a messy divorce. Maybe she'll change, or maybe I can live with these problems." In the end, if the no-nos pose a big enough problem, all the commitment in the world won't be enough to save you. You are going to have to either live with misery or get divorced.

If you buy the wrong dress, you might be out a hundred bucks. If you buy the wrong car, you might be stuck with it for five years. If you end up with the wrong mate, you may have him or her for life, or at least be scarred for life. Why would you impulse-shop for a partner you want to spend the rest of your life with?

Your No-No List Takes The Pressure Off

One mistake I see people make in the search for love, especially women, is that they try so hard to find a mate, they put too much pressure on themselves to perform as the perfect date, perfect girlfriend, or perfect potential mate. Such people tend to also put pressure on everyone they meet who has potential, trying to make these prospects fit their image of "the one." Both parties feel this pressure to the point that they either conform or resist, and end up living a lie or living in conflict. When people give up this high-pressure search for a soul mate, that is usually when they find the right person.

When people act out of desperation, it is never conducive to clear thinking: "I must nab this man, because he's the only one who has been nice to me in two years. If he drives me crazy, so what? We'll just have to work on that." Of course it will not work, because he *will* drive you crazy, and your efforts to make him "work on that" will make him feel unloved. Then comes another ugly breakup.

After a few ugly breakups, some people give up. It is in that surrender that they stop pressuring themselves and others to conform to some preconceived notion of romance. That is the point when they begin to clearly evaluate who is in front of them and whether that person is worth it. One thing you know at that point: you are tired of pretending to be who you are not, and you are tired of settling for less than what you want.

It is when you stop trying so hard that you finally have the wherewithal to observe others, to pay attention to just who other people really are, and who they are not.

Once you let go of your "need" for love, you allow yourself to notice red flags and give yourself time to consider them, to have a little dialogue with yourself: *Is his obsessive attention to detail a quirk or a problem? Is his constant criticism something I can live with? Is he just excitable or is he potentially violent? How important is it?* You are not desperate, so now you have time to ask critical questions and wait to discover the answers before you make a move.

The **No-No List** is a sort of surrender list. It says, "I am not desperate, so I can take my time to consider what I truly want and, more importantly, what I don't want." You are giving up on forcing a relationship to happen. You are open to only making a move when it is right for you, or rather, when you are sure it is not wrong for you.

Why is "giving up" the key? Because when you are not actively pursuing someone or recruiting someone to your personal matchmaking cause, you let your guard down and you try to find out the whole truth about each prospect, including all the reasons for not pursuing or recruiting someone. You are not in the mentality of, "I have to make this work," so you are free to ask the question, "Can this really work?"

When you start asking questions about a potential relationship instead of trying to force it to fit a preconceived notion of what you want, that is when you are more observant. As you surrender looking for the perfect and open yourself to discovering what is imperfect, you also free yourself to let go of your ingrained relationship patterns. You are no longer automatically going for the sexy bad boy or the sensitive mama's boy, the nurturing nice girl or the exciting mean girl. You have a list to remind you, "I know what I don't want." You shut off your autopilot and pay attention to what people actually do.

When you have a **No-No List,** you are not pressured to put up with the negatives just because the positives fulfill some preconceived fantasy. You are liberated from fantasy expectations and free to observe reality.

Chapter 4

X X X ✓

You Are Never
Too Young or Too Old

Never Too Old for a No-No List

You might think you are too old for a **No-No List** because experience has already taught you what to look for, and you learned the hard way! I promise you this: you are never too old to benefit from a **No-No List.**

One thing I have noticed in both clients and friends is that older people are sometimes more receptive to considering the idea of a **No-No List.** Older clients have been around long enough to notice patterns in their relationships. They have begun to realize that their instincts have always spoken to them from the start, but they have not always known how to pay attention to those instincts in an effective way. Your instincts might say, "Something about this guy is off," or "I can't put my finger on it, but I don't trust this woman." You have not identified it yet, but your subconscious could be recognizing a trigger from your past experiences.

You might think that your instincts combined with the wisdom of experience will help you just fine without a list, but awareness does not equal change.

Humans are, by nature, creatures of habit. We tend to repeat patterns because they are familiar. When you make your **No-No List**, you are going to clearly see the negative patterns that repeat in your relationships. You will see them because they are bound to show up as no-nos. What's more, you will begin to learn how these patterns have caused your relationships to repeatedly fail. You will learn this because one requirement for making an effective **No-No List** is to define why your no-nos bother you. The good news is, if you act on your **No-No List**, you can escape your negative patterns!

It can be tempting to think, "That relationship didn't work because he was a jerk," or "We never made it because she was a piece of work." There is a lot of name calling when relationships break up. Although it is easy to blame someone—whether you blame the other person or yourself—that is just not productive. Instead of trying to decide who was at fault, the **No-No List** makes it clear: you simply have not picked the right person yet. The **No-No List** will also reveal that the reason you picked the wrong person is not because you are flawed, but because you simply did not realize there was more than one question to consider.

Remember, the big question is not only, "What do I want?" but, more importantly, "What *don't* I want?"

Older daters tend to already have a few no-nos in mind, but if they do not make and use a **No-No List,** it can be all too easy to end up with the wrong person again. This happens because of something I said a moment ago: awareness does not equal change. You might tell yourself, "I don't ever want to end up with a complainer again," only to end up with exactly that! We gravitate toward the familiar, even when it drives us crazy. Why? Because our primal brain knows we have survived it before, so it is just not sending us running as fast as it should. This happens more frequently in middle-aged daters because of a greater fear: the fear of ending up alone. I see a lot of middle-aged people who are desperate to find a relationship, too desperate for their own good. Men do not seem to worry about this as much as women, because society still unfairly favors the dating older man over the dating older woman.

Whether you are a man or a woman, middle age can frighten you into making bad choices. If you are in a hurry to find a relationship, then you are still better off with a **No-No List,** which will help you find a better partner faster. Think about the possible alternative. Do you really want to have your heart broken again at 40? 50? 60? As we age, knowing what we *don't want* should be more important than ever.

If you are old enough to know what you don't want, then you might be wondering: why write it down? This is not vastly different from goal setting. Multiple studies have shown that people are more likely to achieve goals when they write them down. You might know what you don't want, but the act of writing it down, reading it, understanding it, memorizing it, and living by it is much like practicing that proverbial fire drill over and over. It is your way of ensuring that all those subconscious, reactive parts of your brain are on board with your rational brain, ensuring that your brain is ready to put your experience to work for you. If you are older, you may have been picking the wrong people for a long time now, so you will need to make a much more conscious effort to break the cycle. Your **No-No List** constitutes that conscious effort.

Never Too Young for a No-No List

You might think you are too young for a **No-No List** because you are not ready to limit yourself like that. Maybe it sounds too cynical to you. There is no question we do want different things at different points in our lives. A twenty-year-old wants different things from a relationship than a thirty-year-old does. Similarly, a thirty-year-old might not know as much as a forty-year-old about what he or she does *not* want. However, although our likes and dislikes shift over time, our core values tend to stay relatively stable. Those core values form the basis of what we don't want. Our core values dictate our no-nos. So you are never too young to start making your **No-No List**.

Yes, your **No-No List** might look a bit different in your twenties than it does in your thirties. That idea might make you worry that your **No-No List** will lead you to pick the wrong partner in your twenties or thirties, only to be stuck with him or her when your likes and dislikes change in your thirties or forties. I cannot stress enough that this is the very reason it is worth making your list *now*. The problem is not so much that people's no-nos change over time, but that they typically do not stop to consider the question until a pattern of failed relationships forces them to. One big reason we want different things at thirty or forty than we do at twenty is that we have learned some hard lessons. You can avoid some of the harshness of those lessons by deciding earlier what is important enough to you to draw a boundary; what means enough to you to say no.

Whatever mistakes you might make in youth by not being sure of exactly what you do and don't want will be compounded by giving it no thought at all.

Your likes and dislikes may change over time, but not in the most fundamental ways. If anything, many of the things that drive you to create boundaries in your life will only strengthen as you grow older. So make your list now, and watch how much faster you grow and how much more quickly you find people who are good for you, as opposed to those of your contemporaries who lead the unexamined life.

One thing worth considering is that the behaviors that bug you most in other people now are likely to stay the same or get worse as time goes on. People who exhibit those behaviors are unlikely to change the core values and personality traits that cause them to act that way. Meanwhile, you are unlikely to change the core values and personality traits that make it difficult for you to tolerate those issues.

When you are twenty-five, you might not make much of the fact that someone is a lousy tipper, maybe because you do not see it as a major matter in the grand scheme of things, and even if it is, you are not ready for marriage anyway. But as you project into the future, it is helpful to understand that this sort of behavior may indicate a deeper frugality or even stinginess that could be important to you in a long-term relationship. A person who is a tightwad at twenty-five might simply embarrass you, but a person who is a tightwad at forty-five might cause serious problems in your marriage. On the other hand, a person who is thrifty at twenty-five might embarrass you, but a person who is a wise saver at forty-five might be just the person you want to help support you and your family.

What We Hate About Them Won't Change

When I was younger, I thought I would be able to change some of my husband's ways that drove me crazy. I became much happier in my marriage when, after years of beating my head against a wall, I gradually let go of my futile effort to change him. I now realize that some of the things that drive me nuts about him, and vice versa, are actually differences in our approaches to life, which end up complementing one another.

I did have a **No-No List** of sorts before I got married, though I didn't call it that then. Even though I was very young, I knew there were things I didn't want in my life. My **No-No List** had five items on it:

My First, Unwritten No-No List
1. No addiction
2. No violence
3. No verbal abuse or foul language
4. No cheating
5. No taking me away from my family

I told him about Number 5 more or less like this: I pointed and said, "See my family? They will always be in my life." He has had many occasions to laugh at that last one over our forty years together. He jokingly says to my family, "My God, if I had only known what that meant, I might have backed out." In reality, he accepts and respects my family, and they are intricately woven within our lives, for better or worse.

When I married my husband, I already knew that none of the non-negotiables on my list were likely to be an issue—even though I did not think of them in those terms at the time. Although I had not written a **No-No List**, my husband passed the test on my mental no-nos.

It was characteristics my husband had that I did not pay attention to that subsequently led to our early struggles. As it turns out, my husband is a perfectionist and, as a result, a procrastinator. Me? I make up my mind to do something, and I do it, no hesitation. He usually won't make a move until he has studied something from every angle. For years, that sort of waiting made me nervous, so much so that I would often take over decisions myself. I then would resent him because I assumed he was the one putting that weight on my shoulders. I would nag him to do things, and finally sigh, "I guess I'll have to do it myself."

Eventually I came to realize that even though my husband proceeds only after much deliberation, he always gets things done on time—not in the time I would do it, but still on time. I finally told myself, "Who put you in charge of your husband? Just agree on a deadline and back off. Let him do it in his own way." That was when I realized that the problem I thought *he* had, being a procrastinator, was the flip side of the problem *I* had, being a control freak.

My problem made sense; as an immigrant, I had faced many upheavals that made me feel as if the rug could be pulled out from under me at any moment. This general fear resulted in a powerful, propelling need to always control my circumstances.

Finally I realized that my husband and I are not one person

but two partners. Just because we are married does not mean he is going to become more like me, or vice versa. Consequently, I no longer nag, saying things like, "Honey, did you write that check? Why do you always wait until the last minute?" He is an adult, he knows when the bill is due, and he always pays it on time.

All my efforts to change him only frustrated both of us. I was the one who had to change, not by becoming someone different from who I am, but by letting him be who he is. I will always feel a need for control, and he accepts that too. He understands that my need to make sure everything gets done in a timely and orderly fashion can be a positive trait, just as I know that his need to take his time and make sure he is doing things right can be equally beneficial. For my husband and me, our no-nos were not deal breakers.

For some couples they might be.

I recently counseled a couple who had not been seeing each other all that long. Already they had come into conflict over the parts of their overlapping rings that did not overlap. He was still going through his second divorce from a much younger woman, and he was not sure if he wanted to get into another relationship yet. His new girlfriend, who was also much younger than him, admitted she kept ending up with men who would not commit. Despite all that, they wanted to give it a shot because they came from the same culture and believed they had a lot in common. They were hopeful they could work it out, because they were focused on the 31 percent where they overlapped. I saw doom written all over it, because I was looking at the 69 percent where they did not overlap.

It would be easy for me to make the twice-divorced older man into a bad guy, and he might be. It would be easy for me to say the girl who keeps letting men walk all over her is a ninny, and she might be. Or maybe they just do not know who they are and what they *don't* want. In any case, labeling good guys and bad guys isn't much help in solving the real problem. As the old saying goes, "It takes two to tango."

If a young woman keeps going out with older men who expect her to accommodate all their needs while giving her nothing in return, and if she keeps giving them what they expect, she is going to keep ending up miserable. She is effectively giving up on who she is just to hang on to these guys. Maybe they are bad guys, or maybe they are just more assertive than her, but they are certainly not the right guys for her.

Meanwhile, if an older man keeps going out with younger women because he likes how willing they are to accommodate him, but he finds them childish and unable to think for themselves, he is going to keep ending up miserable. Maybe these women are childish, or maybe they are exactly what they should be for their age and experience, but they are certainly not the right women for him.

This couple needed to stop hanging all their hopes on that 31 percent, and take a hard look at the 69 percent—not just their partner's 69 percent, but also their own. Instead, she kept thinking that if she changed he would change, and he kept thinking that if he refused to change she would have to change. But neither of them was changing. Ultimately, underneath all the changes she struggled to make, she was still the same person, and she could only hide it for so long. She had not really changed, and of course, he had no intention of changing. Without intending to, these two people were living a lie.

Her lie: "If I keep pretending I'm someone else, then he'll become someone else."

His lie: "If I refuse to become someone else, she'll have to become someone else."

But the only people they can ultimately be are themselves. That is never going to change.

Many people want to believe they can solve these issues by changing themselves or changing the other person. Changing yourself or your partner will not do the trick. You cannot change other people; only they can do that, and nobody makes the choice to change just because someone else wants or needs them to change. It is difficult to change things about yourself that go to the roots of your values and ideals without extreme soul searching and possibly therapy, and I don't advise doing it just to please another person. If you do try to change to please somebody else, you will no longer be you. That will inevitably cause you to resent your partner for convincing you to make the real you vanish.

When it comes to the 69 percent of your lives where you and your partner have no common ground, sometimes you can compromise, the way my husband and I did. But that only works if it is not one of your deal breakers. Even then, it is not as much about compromise as it is about surrender. The question is, are you willing to let it go and live with what you perceive as your partner's flaws, as-is?

My husband and I do not overlap any more or less than anyone else. Our relationship works because we *accept* what lies both inside and outside the overlap. One thing that helps is that neither of us is afraid to voice our opinions, whether the other person likes it or not, and neither of us ever punishes the other person for having a different opinion. We might disagree, but we do not make each other pay for it. In the example I gave above, the young woman was afraid: "If I don't agree with him and I don't change myself, I might lose him." She was afraid he would abandon her. So instead she abandoned herself.

If this couple had had the knowledge and the courage to use a **No-No List** before they let it get so far, they could have avoided all the heartache that was coming their way. Their non-negotiable 69 percent really was a deal breaker. There was no way for either of them to surrender what they wanted from each other, without completely surrendering who they were. This is the kind of situation the **No-No List** can help you avoid. Not just because it tells you what you don't want in another person, but also because knowing what you don't want is the beginning to understanding your own values and ideals, the beginning of understanding *who you are*. This is important, because it's not just your partner's 69 percent that's not going to change. Yours won't either.

So if being active is one of the most defining parts of your life, and you cannot coax your new guy or gal off the couch to go on a hike, that's probably the wrong person for you. Maybe you think, "But we have so much else in common and we have great chemistry." Okay, but realize this: that person on the couch is not going to change. You might convince the couch potato to go hiking a few times, but the potato is going to hate it and will ultimately be back on that couch while you're in the woods alone. If you want this to work, you cannot just begrudgingly accept it. You have to *surrender*. You have to decide: "That's who this person is, and I support that this is a terrific person who happens to love reading and watching TV." All the better if you enjoy reading and watching TV, too. Here's the thing: whatever you decide to accept, you have to do so with your eyes open. If you secretly harbor the hope that your partner will change, you're lying to both of you.

Trying to change other people is not good for anyone. If everyone thought they had to become someone other than themselves to find love, the world would become a depressing, repressive place. It is when we support people in blossoming into who they are, including the 69 percent that is completely unlike us, that true love is possible. Why waste time on anything less? It won't yield happy results.

So know your no-nos, and make sure your partner has a **No-No List** as well!

Chapter 5

✗ ✗ ✗ ✓

Make Your No-No List

The List

How do you make your **No-No List**? It is not complicated. You can probably come up with a reasonable list to get you started within just fifteen minutes. However, for your best shot at finding a good match, I suggest you continue to take time to fully develop and refine your list in the weeks and months to come. The list will make you aware of your boundaries in a new way, and each new awareness will lead to another. As you learn those new things, add them to your list.

Certain traits should be on everybody's
No-No List, like *Violence.*

Below, you will find Sample Worksheet #1 (also provided in appendix B for copying), which will get you started. I suggest you use this worksheet as a guide to create a checklist of the traits you are most certain you cannot live with. Add your own no-nos if you don't see them on the worksheet. I believe around ten items is a good number to focus on. That should make your list long enough to be thorough, but short enough for you to commit it to memory. That way you will have it in your head whenever you find yourself in a social situation, making it easier for you to weed out prospects you need to cross off your potential dating list—no matter how tempting they might seem.

Your Worksheet #1 should include three pieces of information:

1. For each No-No, select a word or phrase that provides a shorthand for the trait you don't want.

2. Each No-No should include your own brief definition, a description of what that trait means to you. (The definitions in the sample worksheet are only examples.)

3. For each of your ten No-Nos, use a rating scale of 1 to 10 to rank how important it is to you to avoid someone with that trait. A rating of 1 indicates minimal importance; a rating of 10 indicates critical importance. You do not need to assign each trait a different number. In other words, you can have several items listed as 3s, or 7s, or 10s.

SAMPLE WORKSHEET #1

Table 5.1

No-Nos (Non-Negotiables)	Red Flags/Definitions	Your own definitions	Value to you 1 - 10
Boring	Quiet, does not initiate anything, likes status quo		
Cold mannered	Detached, aloof, disengaged		
Stingy	Does not tip adequately, goes to extremes to save a buck		
Not intellectually stimulating	Does not appreciate challenging books, movies, TV shows, or news programs		
Dependent	Waits for others to decide everything, won't voice likes or dislikes, always relies on others		
Suffocating/ Needy	Wants to always be with you, does not allow room for personal growth, needs constant attention		
Controlling	Wants to tell people what to do all the time, thinks he/she is always right, wants to change everything about you		
Haunted by the past	Lives in the past, cannot get excited about the present or future, makes no room for a new relationship		
Holds a grudge	Remembers the past and won't let it go, not forgiving		

(continued)

No-Nos (Non-Negotiables)	Red Flags/Definitions	Your own definitions	Value to you 1 - 10
Dishonest	Takes pride in fooling other people, lies about age to get discounts, cheats the IRS		
Irresponsible	Does not pay bills on time, does not show up to work on time, does not finish projects, does not keep promises		
Never owns up to mistakes/ Blamer	Never admits being wrong, often blames others for his/her own mistakes, always has an excuse, problems are always somebody else's fault (i.e. in previous relationships)		
Depressed	Downer, pessimistic, always talking about the dark side of things		
Shrewd/ Cunning	Does not stop at anything to get what he/she wants		
Egotistic/ Selfish	It is all about him/her, has to get what he/she wants, ignores the needs of others		
Manipulative	Treats other people as pawns in a game meant to benefit him/ her, always seeks to turn other people's interests or problems to his/her advantage, uses people		

No-Nos (Non-Negotiables)	Red Flags/Definitions	Your own definitions	Value to you 1 - 10
Know-it-all	Never wrong, knows what's best for everybody, grandiose talk or behavior		
Argumentative	Every conversation turns into an argument until you agree with the person		
Temperamental	Constantly screams at or harasses other drivers in traffic, throws a fit in restaurants or stores when service people make mistakes, loses temper whenever things don't go his/her way		
Workaholic	Walks, talks, and breathes nothing but work, does not have a balanced life		
Addiction	Abuses or engages to excess in drugs, alcohol, cigarettes, food, sex, shopping, gambling, etc.; has a generally addictive personality		
Unmotivated	Needs a force behind him/her to get anything done, needs constant coaxing or convincing to pursue goals		
Couch potato	Does not like active life, watches TV more often than any other leisure activity, may also be an introvert		

(continued)

No-Nos (Non-Negotiables)	Red Flags/Definitions	Your own definitions	Value to you 1 - 10
Promiscuous	Makes constant sexual, suggestive, or appraising comments about the opposite sex; brags about previous sexual relationships; does not take commitments seriously; cheats		
Looking for short-term relationship	Long list of previous relationships, lack of commitment		
Lacks loyalty	Talks negatively about family, employer, or friends when they're not present to defend themselves; lack of gratitude		
Competitive	Does anything to win in sports, talks about coworkers as if they're enemies, vies for attention, always needs to get the credit, can't work well in a group		
Perfectionist	Everything has to be organized, cannot stand departing from routine, nothing is ever good enough, never satisfied with self, never quits trying to improve self and world		
Victim mentality	Behaves or speaks as if the world is out to get him/her, "poor me" attitude		

No-Nos (Non-Negotiables)	Red Flags/Definitions	Your own definitions	Value to you 1 - 10
Sexist	Expresses that women/men are only good at certain things, expresses that women/men are incapable of certain things, complains when the opposite sex does something that falls outside gender norms or stereotypes (i.e. men should be handy around the house, men should not cry, women should cook, women should not be in charge)		
Violent	Should be on everybody's list		
Religion mismatch			
Social class mismatch			
Cultural mismatch			
Lack of financial security/ wealth			

Transfer your selected ten or so traits, their definitions, and their importance ratings onto Worksheet #2, which you will find below. List them according to priority, from highest to lowest numerical ratings. As you read this book, and with more insight, you must continually revise your created Worksheet #2. Each revision of this list will get you closer to knowing and understanding the real you, the suitable partner, and whom you need to avoid. The final Worksheet #2 will become the **No-No List** you use on your new and improved search for romance. This list should be copied and used for each prospect.

Study the definitions you have written on your **No-No List** to train yourself to recognize the red flags that signal when someone is engaging in that attitude or behavior. The definitions you have come up with are your personalized road map to those red flags. The clearer you are with your definitions, the better you will get at recognizing red flags. That is why it is wise to keep revising and refining your **No-No List** as you go. It is perfectly fine to use specific examples of things someone did in the past that upset you or that contributed to the destruction of a relationship. This is not about living in the past, but simply learning from it.

SAMPLE WORKSHEET #2

Table 5.2

No-Nos (Non-Negotiables)	Your own definitions	Value to you 1 - 10	Exhibited red flags	Prospect ranking 1 - 10

Listing No-Nos Is Not Judgmental

I've talked to some people who think they have to say yes to everyone who ever asks them out because "I want to keep all my options open." Really? *Every* option? As adults, we deserve to give ourselves permission to know which options are right for us.

The No-No List is not judgmental. It never asks, "What did you do wrong or what did they do wrong?" Instead, it asks, "What don't you want, and why?"

Sure, sometimes people make a better second impression. But usually when a relationship does not work out, people can go back and recall the first time they saw evidence of the future problem. It is not just that hindsight is 20/20. Those red flags bothered them from the start. But they wanted to keep their options open, or they liked other things about the person and hoped the red flag would not be a big deal. One subtext I often hear underneath all this is that people are afraid of seeming judgmental. This is especially true when it comes to those no-nos that don't seem to bother other people they know, but which they consider deal breakers.

Maybe there are some things we would rather the world did not know about us, or about our likes and dislikes. But you and your life partner are going to discover all of them, whether you like it or not. The level to which you will be in each other's business is unprecedented by any other kind of relationship. So, maybe you do not want the world to know about your secret weird eating habits, or that you think a certain political party is ridiculous, or that you do not believe in God, or that you do believe in God but go to a church that some consider a cult, or that you are grossed out by people who are overweight or too thin. But you cannot be afraid to be honest about such things when choosing a potential mate, because if that person does become your spouse, sooner or later you are going to get caught in your politically incorrect, weird, or opinionated ways.

One of my friends recently said of the **No-No List,** "That's so negative. You should focus on the positive." I think she missed my point. I understand the value of looking at the bright side of things, but there is a reason wedding vows talk about "for better or worse": married couples will encounter both. If we can figure out ahead of time what some of "the worse" might be, we have a better shot at knowing if we really can "take this man, or this woman." Your **No-No List** is a great place to start.

Chapter Six

X X X ✔

Use Your No-No List

Observe Before You Date

You will make the best use of your **No-No List** if you can observe potential mates before you date. It is easier to find out who passes your no-no test if you can observe people in their natural environment to see how they interact in different situations with a variety of people. Your opportunity for objective observation is diminished on a typical date, because people on a date are usually on their best behavior. You want to see what they are like when their guard is down. The idea here is that you have not targeted anyone specific yet, so it is unlikely to be on anyone's agenda to impress you. You need to put yourself out there in social situations where you can observe a variety of people and discover which ones you have chemistry with. Then you can check the behaviors and attitudes of prospective candidates against your **No-No List**.

When people hang out with friends or those with whom they share common interests, they are more likely to be themselves. That is when you can make a relaxed study of them.

Some no-nos are not easy to see at first. That's one reason to take the opportunity to observe someone in a neutral setting over time before trying a first date. My son was lucky that he met his wife through a group of young people who pursued recreational sports. They played games like volleyball, soccer, and softball every weekend. That environment let him see what she was like, by spending time getting to know her as a friendly acquaintance. Because they were in an interactive social situation, he had a chance to observe the topics she enjoyed, the way she treated other people in various circumstances, her sense of fair play, the strength and proportion of her ego, her ability to keep commitments, and more. He waited a year to ask her out.

It would have been even easier for my son if he'd had a **No-No List**. As it was, he had plenty of time to consider factors beyond chemistry. The **No-No List** often reveals that the people you consider your "type" are getting between you and your chance to find your soul mate.

Becoming an Effective Observer

Do not carry your **No-No List** around with you or question dating prospects about the items on your list. That is not going to give you accurate results. You need to simply observe. Then wait until you go home to evaluate someone's potential by measuring it against your list.

If you start dating someone before you have made this sort of evaluation, it is unlikely that the person will reveal himself fully to you until after you are hooked, and that is often too late. When someone is on a date, that person won't talk about how much he or she loves to play the field. On the other hand, if that same person is hanging out with a comfortable social group, then it won't be taboo for him or her to look at or comment about other people of interest. That is when you can begin to read that person's attitude and values about dating, and about many other things. When you observe people in a casual group, you can see how much they drink, hear what is important to them in conversation, get a sense of how they participate in activities, and learn how they deal with conflict.

Seek social situations with groups that allow you to encounter some of the same people on a regular basis in a casual way. Seek opportunities for conversation with the person you are interested in. Do not interrogate or barrage that person with questions. That can seem pushy and desperate and will not gain you the information, or the interest, you want. But if, say, the subject of business comes up, people always reveal themselves over the course of a conversation through little telltale signs. If you pay attention to what they say, you can tell who is cutthroat in approaching competition, believing that the end justifies the means. If that trait is on your **No-No List**, this person is not for you. On the other hand, maybe you believe that sometimes a small evil is necessary to do a greater good. If so, maybe he or she is perfect for you.

Some people say you should not date where you work, but let's be realistic: the workplace is an easy place to meet likeminded people, and it is tough to resist when the perfect person happens to work with you. One definite no-no is dating people who have power over you or whom you have power over. Stay away from them or you might kill your career. In other situations, simply vet the person against your **No-No List** before you take the plunge. If the individual you are interested in matches too many of your no-nos, then you are asking for trouble when the inevitable breakup comes and you still have to see her or him daily. Talk about awkward!

If approached properly, the great thing about the workplace is the opportunity to observe people in an environment where they cannot keep their guard up at all hours. You actually can observe before you date. If you are attracted to someone at your workplace, you will have an opportunity to observe how that person treats people who have more power or less power, how he responds to the boss, how she deals with the janitor, how he treats customers on the phone, how she talks about people when they are not around.

It can tell you a lot about someone if you say, "Hi, how are you?" and that person takes it as a cue for a gripe session about customers or fellow employees who are not around to defend themselves. Such behavior could be a red flag if "gossipy" or "victim mentality" is on your **No-No List**. If your dating prospect belittles the janitor, and your **No-No List** mentions "bullying," you might want to reconsider. If your prospect is condescending to the boss, and "lack of judgment" is on your list, keep an eye on that. If Mr. or Ms. Maybe teases colleagues, you might find the jokes witty and inclusive, or you might need to check your **No-No List** for "sarcastic" or "mean." Making these distinctions requires the kind of observation you cannot make on one date.

Applying the No-No List To Your Observations

How do you measure a person's behavior against your **No-No List**? In general, you will still seek potential dates much the way many people do: look for someone you feel attracted to and talk with that person to find out what you have in common. But before you decide to go on a date, go a step further: seek as many opportunities as possible to observe that person in neutral social situations to learn more. I recommend you find at least half a dozen opportunities to get to know a prospect around other people before you ever go on a one-on-one date.

With the **No-No** method of vetting potential mates, the way you decide whether or not to go on that first date may change. Your initial **No-No List** is a guide to help you keep your eyes open for the red flags that signal which people are likely to be wrong for you despite your initial attraction. However, once you meet someone who interests you so much that you wish to consider pursuing that interest further, it is time to make an individualized **No-No List** for that person. Make sure to do this exercise before you ask that prospect out on a date or accept that prospect's request for a date.

Making that second, individualized list is a critical step in this process. Don't skip it just because you have already made your original list.

During the observation stage, you are going to use Worksheet #2, filled out with your selected no-no traits, to see how people measure up against your **No-No List**. When people ask you out, you are going to ask to get back to them. On the other hand, if you want to ask them out, you are going to ask for contact info and ask if you can get in touch sometime. Then, that night when you go home, you are going to use your filled-out Worksheet #2 to see how each prospect measures up against your **No-No List**.

How to Use Your Custom Worksheet #2:

1. Make multiple copies of your customized Worksheet #2.
2. Use a separate Worksheet #2 for each dating prospect.
3. Check off the traits from your **No-No List** that you suspect the prospect might have.
4. Describe the red flags that indicate he or she might have those traits.
5. Rank how strongly they appear to exhibit each no-no on a scale of 1 to 10.

Resist the temptation to tell yourself that a red flag is just your imagination, that this person's positive qualities will render those negatives unimportant, or that you can learn to deal with it or the person might outgrow it or that love might inspire the other person to change. The presence of a red flag is almost never your imagination. People will reveal themselves to you, if you just pay close attention to what they say and do. When people reveal negative things about themselves, either directly or indirectly, do yourself a favor: believe them. When you see a red flag, the biggest favor you can do for both yourself and that other person is to run the other way.

After you have filled out a **No-No List** specific to the person you hope to date, a lot of this is common sense. As a rule of thumb, if the prospect has two or more traits that you have rated 5 or higher in your "Value to You" column, and if on those traits the prospect rates 5 or higher in the "Prospect Ranking" column, then I would not suggest a first date. For anything below those lines, I suggest you study your list and decide how important those things are to you in the long term. If you are confident that the person you are interested in has enough going for him or her that you would be able to graciously surrender an item or two on your list, then go on a first date.

Your **No-No List** is not perfect mathematics or exact science. Rating each no-no on a scale of 1 to 10 is helpful in giving you a way to weigh and balance all the pros and cons of a potential relationship. However, at the end of the day you still have to subjectively decide if the way a particular person exhibits a no-no makes it a major deal breaker, a potential problem or challenge, or nothing more than a minor annoyance. How much does it take to tip the scales against deciding to date this person: five small no-nos? one huge no-no? three medium-sized ones? The bottom line question you have to ask yourself is this: "If this behavior never changed, could I live with it?" If not, you should give a thumbs-down to even going on a first date with that person. The reasons will become clearer as you continue reading this book.

If someone asks you out before you have finished with the observation stage, you are going to suggest to the person that you get together a couple more times in neutral social situations directly involving other people: barbecues, hikes, parties, dinners, dancing, etc. Remember, it is important that this is not just the two of you in a crowd of strangers, but among other people you can both interact with. At the very least, request a double date. When you meet on these group occasions, you will continue to learn more about the person. So, when you go home, go through the same exercise again, rating them against your Worksheet #2. Do this for the first few get-togethers. With practice, you will begin to see red flags before it is too late.

Once you become adept at using your **No-No List,** you will be on your way to finding someone who does not present any, or many, red flags.

To give you a clearer idea of how to create your custom Worksheet #2, allow me to tell you Brandy's story and share her custom worksheet with you. You will find out that creating a custom worksheet is not as difficult as you might have thought.

Brandy's No-No Nightmare

A friend of mine—let's call her Brandy—went online dating for a while and reported plenty of horror stories to me. Brandy often said something like, "There was something about this guy that didn't feel right, but I couldn't put my finger on it." Too bad she did not have a **No-No List**. See if you can spot the red flags Brandy missed, now that you have read a bit and are in a **No-No** frame of mind:

After one of Brandy's bad dates, I said, "Describe the entire date from beginning to end."

"First of all," she began, "he was like ten, fifteen minutes late."

I knew my friend well enough to know what this meant. He was already **No-No** City for her. I asked her to explain anyway. They were meeting at a restaurant for lunch. She lived in Austin, Texas, and he lived in Georgetown, nearly thirty miles away.

"So it bothered you that he was late?" I asked.

She replied, "Well, maybe he had a hard time getting there because of traffic, but why didn't he plan for that?"

It was already clear to me that "Tardiness" is a big no-no for Brandy. When I tell her to stop by my house at 7:30, I am not kidding you, it feels as if she is standing on the doorstep with a timer at 7:25, and when it hits 7:30 sharp she is ringing the bell.

I grinned. "Okay. What else?"

"The way he was dressed. He was kind of sloppy. He wore jeans and tennis shoes."

"So you don't like a guy to dress casually?"

"He's going on a date, not to the gym. That's disrespectful."

"Maybe he's just comfortable in his skin."

"I'm comfortable with myself, too, but he should be thinking about me. I cared enough about making a nice impression that I dressed up for him. He should spend a little more time dressing himself. To me that shows that he thinks highly of me, that he thinks I'm worth a little trouble." On that note, another of Brandy's big no-nos might be either "Sloppy" or "Doesn't make an effort," depending on how she views this trait.

"Okay. Then what?"

"Then when he came into the restaurant the first thing he wanted to do was to kiss me. I'm just saying hello and I'm thinking *I don't even know you yet*. It wasn't just a kiss on the cheek, either. He tried to kiss me on the mouth."

"Okay, you don't want somebody who is too forward?"

"Right. It's disrespectful."

During their lunch, things continued to go downhill. He told her, "Since I've never been in this restaurant, why don't you pick something for me?" This irked her because she had no idea what he liked, and when she asked him it took forever to get him to give her some idea of his taste in food. After much deliberation, she finally picked something for him, and then when his food arrived he complained about it. This was definitely a red flag for her: The guy could not make his own decisions, and he seemed likely to blame other people for the results.

"If he was going to be so picky, then he should pick his own food," she said.

She said that their conversation over lunch actually had some interesting moments. Then he started badmouthing his ex-wife. His ex was to blame for everything: she took his kids away, she was a control freak, she was selfish . . . "Everything was whine, whine, whine." For Brandy, this verified the red flag about blaming other people for his problems.

The coup de grace? "When we were leaving he says, 'I can follow you home.' So I say, 'I don't know you from Adam! This is the first time we've met. You're not going to my home.'"

Two years later I asked Brandy to help me with an experiment: "I want you to go back to that terrible date and create a **No-No List** for me." Every one of those things I predicted was high on her list, including the biggest hot button: she did not want someone who showed up late. For Brandy, poor time management was a sign of disrespect for other people's time. I see this problem a lot with couples. It creates anxiety for the punctual partner, because that person is forced to wait, uncertain that the other person will show up.

Being fifteen minutes late to a first date might be a minor issue, but it can become a major issue later in a relationship. For example, men sometimes have to wait for women to get ready, which can cause fights before social events because people are anxious about losing face. Or maybe they share a ride to work and argue because *he* is always late, which can cause fights over the potential repercussions from their employers. Couples who are at odds on this subject have a big problem. The fear comes up every time: "Is my partner going to fail me again?"

For Brandy, tardiness had an underlying meaning of disrespect, so she decided to put "Disrespect" on her list as its own individual no-no.

I said, "Explain respect to me."

She said, "When they promise to do something, I expect them to keep that promise."

So on her **No-No List**, she would write, "Disrespect." Then she would define that as: "Doesn't keep promises. Breaks commitments. Not dependable. Doesn't make effort to show I'm important, such as being on time or looking nice for me."

There is no one-size-fits-all No-No List.

Brandy's list would look very different from mine. Not only would tardiness not bother me in a man, but somebody who is fussy about punctuality would be a no-no for *me*. In my culture, when you say the party is at 7:30, people do not show up until 8:30 or 9:00. But if I invite Brandy at 7:30, she will be ringing the bell at 7:30, when I am stepping in the shower. I learned how to make this work in my relationship with Brandy. If I invite people over for a party at 7:30, I tell Brandy to come at 8:30. That way I know they will all arrive at the same time. On the other hand, if just Brandy and I are getting together, I set my personal schedule an hour earlier to make sure I am on time.

Brandy told me that she is aware that some might consider her insistence on punctuality uptight. Good, she knows herself. So if Brandy meets a man who has "perfectionist" or "uptight" on his **No-No List**, he might need to cross her off his list too.

I was especially interested in what the no-no was when Brandy's date tried to kiss her right away, and to go home with her on her first date. She said, "That's not how you treat a lady!" That might go under "Disrespect": "Doesn't treat me like a lady." However she might also want to give "Treats me as a sex object" a separate listing, because all of her hot buttons go back to disrespect, which is a core value for her. This might seem like an obvious no-no to some people, but the point is that it has a special meaning for her and she needs to understand what that is. Other people don't have the same boundaries about sexuality.

Years ago I asked some new friends, "How did you two meet?" I was surprised by the answer. She said they met at a party where it was love at first sight, so they ended up at her home that same night and did not leave her house for three days. Some may wonder, "How could she go home with a man she just met?" That is not how they saw it: sure, the chemistry was there, but they also found out all about each other as they talked during those three days. For them, time was not a factor in deciding what they felt certain about quickly. They knew they were meant for each other. They got married a month later, and it lasted. For them, those three days did not constitute being treated as a sex object. That phrase would not show up on their **No-No Lists** in the first place, because it is not an issue in their way of viewing the world.

The beauty of the **No-No List** is that it allows you to cut to core issues right away. Brandy was so turned off by her online date that she did not need a list to know he was wrong for her, but what if there had been chemistry between them? She might not have heeded the warning signs of trouble. Or what if she missed a cue? What's more, it would have been so much easier if she could have used a **No-No List** in a more neutral social situation where she would not have had to fend off his embarrassing advances.

Brandy's story is one of many that have convinced me to arm more people with the **No-No List**. Now that you are familiar with the worksheet, you can look at Brandy's and tell right away that her date holds too many no-nos: six that she rates 7 or higher in importance.

Do not worry if you are still not sure of the steps to make your No-No List. Appendix A at the end of the book will remind and guide you through the steps.

Brandy's Worksheet #2

Table 6.1

No-Nos (Non-Negotiables)	Your own definitions	Value to you	Exhibited red flags	Prospect Ranking
Abusive	Verbal or physical abuse	10	N/A	-
Disrespectful	Punctuality, keeping promises, attention to appearance, treating me as sex object	10	Sloppy dresser, wanted to kiss me and go home with me, was late and not even apologetic for it	10
Not intellectually stimulating	Not well read, not well educated, does not follow politics	10	He is not well read, conversation was very superficial	8
Controlling	Controls what I should wear, say, eat or do; controls me financially	10	N/A	-
Suffocating	Does not allow personal space or time	10	N/A	-
Not well to do	Should be wealthy enough, should be able to financially support himself, must have a good-paying job	9	He does not have a good-paying job	8

(continued)

No-Nos (Non-Negotiables)	Your own definitions	Value to you	Exhibited red flags	Prospect Ranking
Blamer	Blames others for his misfortunes, does not own up to his mistakes and actions	9	Blamed his wife, blamed me for the choice of food	7
Dishonest	Lacks integrity	8	N/A	-
Victim mentality	The world is after him, poor me attitude, does not take responsibility	8	Talked bad about his wife, blamed her for all wrongs	7
Indecisiveness	Cannot make up his mind, cannot make a timely decision, is not willing to participate in decision making	7	Could not order his food and was not even willing to participate in this process	7
Argumentative	Must be able to agree to disagree	6	N/A	-
Holds a grudge	Will not let go of the past	6	Constantly talked about the ex-wife and how horrible she was	6

Now that I have walked you through the process of creating Brandy's worksheet, I suggest you take this opportunity to put what you've learned to use. This would be a good time to check your own list and see if it can use some revising.

Online Dating and Other Obstacles to Observation

Although it is easier to use the **No-No List** if you can observe someone before dating, it can also be useful for online or blind dating. In fact, the list becomes more critical if you must meet with someone you have only gotten to know online or through a friend's recommendation.

The problem that online or blind dating poses is that online sites, and friends, tend to match you with somebody with whom you have plenty in common, but they cannot reveal to you how a person will behave in a real situation. Sure, some dating-site questionnaires pose hypothetical questions about values, but while a few people might be honest enough to say, "I have a temper" or "I'm sexually open," it's unlikely someone will admit "I throw things when I'm angry" or "I'm addicted to porn."

Online dating sites make it too easy to present a perfect picture and hide the real person. There is nothing wrong with wanting to make a good impression. Finding the right partner is not just about finding someone you want by your side in good times, but also about finding someone you want by your side in bad times. You will not know that until you can observe this person at his worst moments. You are not trying to find out whether this person is perfect all the time, but rather whether his or her imperfections are of a sort you can live with. Your **No-No List** will help you find the red flags and decide how important they are.

The early phase of online dating requires nothing but a barrage of words and photos. No vocal intonation, social inter-action, body language, facial expressions, actions, reactions, or nonverbal cues. Most communication is not contained in words, but in all those other things.

Most people won't reveal red flags online.

You are hardly going to find out how someone ranks on your **No-No List** through personality profiles, messaging, or emails. You can only pick up on negatives by observing the other person in the course of social interactions, both in terms of behavior toward you and behavior toward others. If he makes you laugh all night, but tosses back five Scotches in one sitting, you might want to see if addiction is on your **No-No List**. If she's sweet to you all throughout dinner, but treats the waiter like a slave and browbeats him for a simple mistake, then you might want to check your **No-No List** for "Snob," "Impatient," or "Cruel."

Online dating is a great place to weed out people who don't overlap with you in areas you hope to have in common. But even in a best-case scenario, the area of your two lives in which you share things in common will hover around 31 percent. You still have to figure out what's going to happen when you encounter the 69 percent you don't have in common. That requires recognizing red flags. You can begin to ferret out some of those when you begin messaging, emailing, and phoning potential dates. But you might not find out much until you get to that first meeting. In either case, how will you know what a red flag looks like if you have never given a thought to what you don't want? This is where the **No-No List** comes into play.

When you use the **No-No List** for online dating, everything starts the same as usual. I suggest your first few meetings take place in as broad a social context as possible, with an opportunity to interact with plenty of other people. This will allow you to observe as much communication as possible. But if you are like most online daters, you will first meet over coffee or drinks. The **No-No List** can still be effective in that situation too, so long as you understand that your old dating approach needs to change.

Online dating all starts with the unspoken question: "Are you a possible match?" But once you meet, you must switch to a new unspoken question: "Are you a possible No-No?"

You need to be just as eager to find out whether someone is *not* "the one" as you are to find out whether someone *is* "the one." Watch how the other person acts, but more importantly how the other person interacts—not just with you but also with other people. If you have studied your **No-No List** before the date and you take a good look at it again afterward, you will be able to hone your radar for picking up those clues that will help you not only figure out who might be right for you, but also whom you want to avoid on the way to Mr. or Ms. Right.

Chapter 7

X X X ✔

Know a No-No
When You See One

Draw Your Lines

Your **No-No List** only provides you with guidelines, not hard-and-fast rules. The list serves as a reminder for you to establish and maintain boundaries that reflect your authentic self. You do so by drawing lines in the sand that mark the edges of your boundaries: those are your no-nos.

It is up to you how strict to be about maintaining the lines you draw. They may range from "approach with caution" to "cross at own risk" to "do not cross at any time."

It is important to be clear about what you don't want. However, no matter how detailed you make your **No-No List,** it will always deal with broad ideas: personality and character traits, behaviors and habits, expressions of personal values and traditions. You are bound to see such human qualities in a subjective light. The trick is figuring out what red flags in a potential date should set off an alarm, alerting you to possible trouble in the future. You are the arbiter of what constitutes a red flag, because you are the one who will have to live with the consequences.

Still, I do want to offer you a few examples. In this chapter, we will take a closer look at a few of the sample no-nos I suggested in Worksheet #1. As we do so, we will consider how someone might recognize theoretical no-nos in real-life situations. Please do not limit yourself to the examples here. I suggest you also come up with your own no-no labels, and define your own red flags, because each individual experiences these issues differently.

Dishonest:

When I use the word *dishonest*, I am thinking about the type of person who takes pride in fooling others, who lies about his or her age to get a discount, who lies to the IRS and considers it a justifiable means to an end instead of calling it fraud. If *dishonesty* is a hot button for you, how can you recognize it in someone you do not yet know well? Most people who are comfortable with dishonesty assume others think like them. It is not hard to catch them bragging about something they gained through dishonest means, or to spot them in a dishonest act.

You will be surprised what people reveal about themselves if only you give them the opportunity.

Sometimes dishonesty initially shows up in little ways. Maybe a dating prospect uses an outdated student ID to get a discount at a movie. Maybe that is no big deal to you. The problem is, if they are willing to reveal that to you before they know you well, then it might only be the tip of the iceberg. Maybe it is more than that: a sales clerk accidentally charges your prospect five dollars for a ten-dollar item, and the prospect says nothing to the clerk but brags to you about getting a big discount. Maybe you are okay with that, too, but I doubt it will stop there.

What if a new friend confides that she fooled her insurance company? Say her basement flooded and she pretended that a few more things used to be down in the basement than actually were, including a TV that was already broken before the flood. This person is proud of outsmarting the insurance company and believes she deserves a break after all the bad breaks she has had. Maybe you would applaud her too. Perhaps what I see as dishonest you see as street smart. If so, maybe dishonesty should not be on your **No-No List**. However, if dishonesty is truly a no-no for you, then all of the above examples are red flags.

My son recently put together a concert for the first time. At first he was excited to work with a temporary business partner who knew all about the industry. Call him Mike. "I can learn from Mike," my son said. My son was in charge of financial logistics. When he told Mike the cost of insuring an event for five thousand people, Mike put up a fight, demanding that my son tell insurers only three hundred were attending. My son made it clear that he considered that foolish and refused to lie, especially considering the potential liabilities at an event involving a huge crowd, live entertainment, and alcohol. Luckily my son had the final say. After a few similar run-ins, he will never do business with Mike again. Dishonesty is a big no-no for my son.

You can use your No-No List to gauge all kinds
of relationships, not just romantic ones.

Whether a prospective date, mate, or partner justifies defrauding the IRS or simply fooling a local mom-and-pop store, the reality is that if somebody tells you the ends justify the means, then this attitude will invade every aspect of your relationship. It will ultimately impact you. If you excuse it now, you will regret it later. Do not ignore the signs.

Cold:

When I use the word *cold* in relation to the **No-No List**, I am referring to people who rarely show emotion. I am an affectionate person who is open about expressing feelings, whether verbally with loving words, or physically with hugs and kisses. My son is a grown man, but I still squeeze him and kiss him and tickle him as if he were a little boy. If we are around people who are reserved, I do not change my behavior, though I might say, "I'm sorry if it looks wrong to you guys, but to me he's still my baby." I learned that from my father.

I remember my father hugging and kissing all of us a lot when I was a child, saying "I love you," laughing and teasing, offering heartfelt advice, and bestowing compliments. My mother, on the other hand, has always been reserved. I love her very much, and I know she loves me, but in terms of the **No-No List** I would describe her as cold. She is more of an organizer and controller, and to achieve that she often speaks her mind but holds back her emotions.

My husband's father came from a military background and to me he seemed cold, dry, and rigid. His mother is similar. They are not demonstrative. The first time my husband saw me, I was eighteen. I walked into my house, rushed over to my dad where he sat in front of the TV, and gave him a hug. Then Dad said, "Give daddy a kiss," so I gave him a big kiss. I recall that my future husband, whom I had no idea I was going to marry, looked embarrassed.

Shortly after our wedding, we took a trip to visit my in-laws. One night after dinner, my father-in-law was seeing to my comfort, and his kindness gave me an urge to grab his cheeks and say an affectionate, "Goochi goochi goo!" like I sometimes did with my father. The whole room fell into stunned silence. Then my father-in-law burst out laughing and everyone relaxed. Later my husband explained that none of them had ever dared do anything like that to his father, and that his acceptance of such a show of affection was a surprise.

I have always been affectionate with my husband, and he likes the attention, though sometimes it was a bit much for him early in our marriage. I think he enjoys the loving words and gestures he missed as a child. Even though he is more reserved than I am, I would not consider him a cold person. If he were, that would be a no-no for me. He has even learned to be affectionate with our son, hugging him and saying, "I love you." Some of that has been due to my influence. It did not come easily to him, but only because he was not accustomed to it. It did not take a lot to convince him. That is not possible with truly cold people.

What are the signs that indicate a cold person? If "Cold" is on your **No-No List**, be leery of people who avoid talking about personal subjects, who act embarrassed or annoyed when others talk about their feelings, who rarely hug people, who flinch when people touch them.

You might think, "But he looks at me in a special way he doesn't share with anyone else, so I know he loves me," or "She had a hard childhood, and I want to make it up to her," or "This person will warm up when we know each other better." Don't count on it. Cold people might have good reasons for being that way, but such behavior tends to be ingrained. If it changes, the pace is liable to be glacial. If you are affectionate, this person probably won't meet your needs.

If you fail to heed early warning signs, you may face a lonely life down the road. Being in a relationship with someone who will not demonstrate love can be lonelier than living alone.

I often hear people, women particularly, saying that a spouse or significant other is difficult to get to know, does not share feelings, or keeps things bottled inside. This makes them feel isolated, neglected, or abandoned. Why take one step down that road? The standoffish person might strike you as a challenge, but when you tire of the challenge, you will be left in the cold. If "Cold" is on your **No-No List**, avoid people who hold themselves at a distance. Seek people who show warmth, hold your gaze, accept a touch on the arm, hug their friends, play with children, kiss their mothers, and tell their fathers, "I love you." Seek people who share revealing stories without apology, within reason of course. What is reasonable? That is up to you.

Stingy:

I was part of a group that regularly met for dinner, and one of the couples in that group provides an example of how you can identify warning signs of the no-no of *stinginess*. For our outings, at first we paid with separate checks. This couple was wealthy enough that they could afford to order whatever they wanted, but they would just order a salad to share and drink water.

When our group grew, the restaurant was unwilling to provide separate checks. We decided that, rather than doing the math to divide the check, we would split the bill evenly. This meant that one night a few people might pay extra, but another night they would pay less, so we figured it would come out relatively even in the end. That's when the Salad Couple changed eating habits. Now that the bill was split ten ways, they began eating lobster, steak, and other expensive items. It seemed they decided that if they had to split costs they might as well get the most out of it. They always ate at a discount because the rest of us picked up the slack.

The Salad Couple did not stop there. If the bill broke down to seventy dollars a couple, it would turn out they only had sixty. "Sorry, I don't have a ten," the husband might say. So someone would offer to throw in a ten. "Thanks, I owe you." But he never paid it back and it soon happened again, and again.

If you have your eye on a dating prospect among a group of people you hang out with, if one of your no-nos is "Stingy," and if that prospect pulls any of the Salad Couple's tricks: beware. You can be sure the stinginess will not stop the minute you leave the restaurant.

Please do not mistake me on this one. I am not talking about someone who is careful with money, for example someone who suggests a less expensive restaurant because he is on a budget or someone who orders salads because she likes salads. A person who leaves a small tip one time might simply have made a mistake on the math, but if she does it two or three times or if he declares he does not believe in tipping, you start to form a picture of that person's values.

You need to pay close attention to get
a feel for patterns of behavior.

Please do not feel bad if you find the Salad Couple thrifty rather than stingy. That probably means "Stingy" is not on your **No-No List**. That is not to say you are stingy. You simply have more tolerance for a wider range of behavior in this area. One important thing to remember is that the Salad Couple found each other. Whether you find such people miserly or economical, there are others out there who think like you. The point is that if "Stingy" is on your list, the signs will be there for you to read, so long as you keep your eyes and ears peeled.

Dependent:

Dependency is easy to define, but it is not as easy to spot as some of the other possible no-nos. Dependent people usually do their best to project confidence in public because they have been conditioned to do so. But, if you pay close attention, you will spot them.

Dependent people show this trait in many different ways, such as: they cannot make decisions on their own, they wait for someone else to approve everything they do, they need another person to do everything for them. They might be financially dependent or emotionally dependent, but they make it clear that without another person in their lives, they are lost.

You might wonder, "How can I know if someone is like that before we are in a relationship?" In this case, it is important to pay attention to the way they talk about past relationships. Do other people's names come up with regard to every decision they have made? Did she become a born-again Christian while dating person A, only to give that up in favor of Buddhism while dating person B? Did he go for a master's degree because Dad told him to, only to quit grad school when his friend needed help starting a business? These are people who doubt their own minds. Pay attention to how heavily they lean on friends to help them make decisions, from ordering dinner, to choosing a political opinion, to deciding what job to take.

Hints of dependency will pop up even before a romantic relationship begins, because it will be clear they do not know what to do without one. They probably have never found themselves in between committed relationships for long and have never spent much time alone.

It can be tempting to jump into a relationship with someone who highly values your opinion, who wants your company so much, who calls constantly because he or she is so interested in you. Wait, listen, think. This flattering attention may truly be what it seems at first: the overwhelming interest of someone who is falling in love. However, it may be something else entirely: the suffocating need of someone who cannot stand to be alone.

Let me share a couple of examples I've seen of what can go terribly wrong in relationships based on dependency:

One couple I counseled did not identify the dependency issue until after they had been dating for a few years. Charlotte had never been in a long-term relationship before. Joey was divorced. He was the dependent one. At first, every sign of dependence looked to her like a sign of true love. "Oh, my God, he loves me so much that he calls me every day." He was not trying to mislead her. He believed the same thing too.

Charlotte was an independent woman who owned a hair-styling business. She only styled hair three days a week, so she had to pack all the clients she could into those three days. The problem was that Joey refused to eat dinner alone: "I don't like for you to work so late, because I need you to eat with me." So she juggled her schedule for him, costing her clients and stress.

On top of that, whenever Joey's mother came to visit him he insisted that Charlotte stay with him to help defend him against his mother's interference in his life. The mother was a sarcastic woman who often belittled him, and he insisted he could not handle her on his own. "You need to stay with me!" So Charlotte stayed, although the woman was even ruder to her.

It soon became clear this guy could not handle anything alone. Charlotte would stay with him for a few days, but he would never let her out of his sight. Whenever she said that she needed time alone for a few days, all he could hear was that she wanted to abandon him.

Charlotte explained, "I need my space. I can't go to the bathroom without you knocking on the door. I can't read a book without you interrupting every two minutes. It's just too much."

Joey could not understand. "I'm dying here. It's too lonely without you. I don't want to watch TV alone. I want to share it with you."

When he was cooking he wanted her in the kitchen with him chopping vegetables, so they could be together. In some relationships, that would be a romantic moment. For Charlotte and Joey it might have been too, if he had ever also allowed her a moment to herself.

What at first seemed lovey-dovey turned out to be a big No-No: he was suffocating her.

Diane and Scott have a different dependency issue. Diane has trouble relying on herself to handle no-nos that come up in her marriage. One night at 10:30, Diane called me in tears because she and Scott were having an argument they could not resolve. The subject was not major, like abuse, infidelity, addiction, or lying. It was his lack of attention to her.

Scott had come home after working a ten-hour shift. He had requested an hour to shower and relax before tending to Diane and the kids. Though Diane agreed to that, she kept showing him some clothes she had bought for the kids that day and asking what he thought of them. Scott, tense from a tough workday, said an abrupt, "They're fine." Diane got upset with his dismissive attitude and insisted on his total attention. Their discussion turned into a huge argument. Scott finally composed himself, gave up on having time to himself, and tried to engage in the conversation his wife wanted. She could not let it end there.

Diane sensed Scott's frustration, and after they put the kids to bed she asked why he was frustrated. He tried to avoid the discussion, knowing from experience that this could turn into an all-night argument. He said he needed to get some sleep to be able to start an early day at work. The more he retreated, the more desperate she became to draw him out.

As Diane put it to me, "He's not willing to listen to me."

I tried to explain, "You and Scott are different. You're the type who wants to talk about problems until they're solved, but Scott needs a couple of days to calm down so he can think about them. He doesn't want to talk to you right now. Nothing you do is going to change that."

She could not accept it. The thought of putting it off only made her cry harder. "I can't hold on to this another day. I won't be able to think or get anything else done until it's resolved."

For Diane, it was a no-no to avoid solving problems. For Scott, it was a no-no to push him when he was overwhelmed.

The biggest problem for Scott was Diane's dependency. You can see it in her dependence on her husband to approve all her choices—such as the children's clothes—as well as her dependence on me to mediate what should have been a simple disagreement. It *is* what I do, but it was not an emergency. It could have waited until our next session. Diane had reached a level of **No-No** that Scott could not tolerate. What Diane was exhibiting in her marriage at that moment was present when they were dating. What intrigued Scott while dating, being a hero to his woman and solving her problems, now felt suffocating.

One of the biggest dangers of dependency is that it often invites someone controlling to take up the other side of the partnership. As far as I am concerned, that sort of codependency, in which one person feeds off of the partner's lack of self-sufficiency while the other feeds off of the partner's need to dominate, is not good for anybody.

If "Dependent" is on your **No-No List**, that does not mean you should avoid people who ask for help. On the contrary. Part of being self-sufficient is being strong enough to admit that we need other people and knowing when to ask for help. This can pose a problem in discerning codependency, because people really do need each other's support to get through life. Sometimes one person or the other is better at something. Maybe he is a better cook and she is a better vacation planner; maybe she is better at juggling bills and he is better at home repairs.

Part of the beauty of marriage is
supporting each other by each bringing
different strengths to the table.

The problems begin when someone cannot make a move on his or her own, when that person needs someone else to make all the decisions, or worse, to do it all. That sort of dependency is a no-no for many people, men and women alike.

Controlling:

It can be easy to get pulled in by someone who is *controlling* before you realize it. That is another reason it is important to spend plenty of time testing prospective dates against your **No-No List** before you go on a first date. Controlling people often use this trait in admirable ways that might throw you off their scent. They can be charismatic leaders who take charge, go-getters with ambition, heroes who save the day. Controlling people can also be pushy, telling other people how to live their lives; self-righteous, so sure they're always right that they make others wrong; or self-centered, always insisting on their own way. If "Controlling" is on your **No-No List**, then pushy, self-righteous, and self-centered are among the sneaky signals to look for.

A warning sign in controlling people is that when they try to convince you to do what they want, they insist they have your best interests at heart. This makes it hard to say no.

When someone gives advice or makes suggestions, listen carefully. If they are controlling, you will notice that whatever they ask you to do is rarely about you. It is all about them. These people believe they do no wrong, make no mistakes. They know all the answers.

Although controlling people can seem charming at first, the signs are there from the start. Say you dress up for a party and this person says, "That's a nice color on you, but I'd love to see what you look like in a more natural looking material," or "Have you ever thought about wearing your hair up?" Or maybe you offer an opinion on something in a conversation and this person says, "That's what I used to think until I read so-and-so's book. Next time we get together I'll give you a copy. I know you'll love it." Do you see how it seems as if this person is taking an interest in you, yet there is a hint that he or she is invested in getting you to do things differently?

One or two of the above comments might not indicate a controller. With a controller, the pattern will continue. You may notice that this person tries to order your food for you, subtly makes you doubt yourself in conversation, or insists on doing things for you that you would rather do yourself. A controller may try taking over every decision, without you having much say, or any say: what you wear, how much you spend, whom you talk to, what job to take, how to talk to your boss, how to discipline the kids. In a worst-case scenario, you could end up with someone emotionally or physically abusive who makes you feel like a prisoner in your own life.

Women can be as controlling as men, but let's consider the story of a couple in which the man is controlling and the woman dependent. She is in her forties but still works as a model. She is a knockout. She has breast implants, her hair and makeup are always perfect, nails manicured, clothes impeccable. She never finished high school, but she is intelligent and charming.

A few weeks after they met, they both declared their love. He told her he wanted to marry her. As soon as she was on board with that, he started asking her to change. He had known about her job and her lack of education from the start, but soon he felt compelled to correct or improve many aspects of her life. One major change: he told her she should quit modeling.

He said something like, "Why are you wasting your time on such a stupid job? When you marry me, you're going to get rid of that job and I'm going to send you to college."

That hurt her feelings. "So you think I'm stupid?"

Yes, sometimes she regrets that she never finished her high school diploma, but at this point in middle age she is content with who she is and the job she has. Mind you, I am a big believer in education, and if she wanted to go to college I would say, "Good for you!" But college does not interest her. It is not what she wants. It is what *he* wants. The sad part is that, even though his suggestions for improvement hurt her feelings, she bought into it. "Maybe at my age it's time to consider a different line of work. Maybe it wouldn't hurt to go back to school."

When she reached out to me, I tried to explain that giving in to his demands would not satisfy him. It would only be the beginning. "You can't jump high enough, no matter what you do. Not for somebody who is so controlling. This is always going to be an issue." If she goes to college, he will choose her major. If she gets a degree, he will pick her job. It will never end.

Do not think I am only concerned about *her*. He is not any happier than she is, because by picking women he can control he is picking women who never satisfy him. He has been married three times, and until now he has had a pattern of picking women much younger than himself. Because they are much younger and view him as older and wiser, they are easily influenced.

He complains to me, "I don't like weak women. I always end up with weak women."

"You picked them," I say. "If you don't want weak women, are you prepared to let a woman do what she wants without trying to improve her or tell her how to live?"

He is confused when I say that. He does not realize that is what he is doing. So long as no woman ever stands up to him, he may never see it. He will always see it as the woman's fault. He thinks he is trying to make her stronger by changing her. He does not realize that her willingness to change for him is the source of the weakness he hates. And around it goes.

If you depend heavily on others, the No-No of "Controlling" is a Never-Ever for you. You are in danger of getting run over in a relationship with someone who is controlling.

Identifying no-nos is not difficult in and of itself. It requires you to take your time and not rush to go on that first date until you have all the information. You need time to identify patterns of behavior. Once you recognize the patterns, your challenge is to remain realistic about what you discover. You do yourself a disservice when you rationalize the other person's behavior. As poet Maya Angelou said, "The first time someone shows you who they are, believe them."

I hope the examples in this chapter have offered you insight into how to put your **No-No List** to use. They may also have helped you rethink your priorities. If so, this is another good time to fine-tune your **No-No List** to reflect your growing understanding of yourself.

Chapter 8

X X X ✔

No-Nos Reveal Who You Are

You Can't Always Know What You Want

I have a friend who divorced many years ago. She and her ex-husband both worked in the same field, had plenty of interests in common, and had three children together. As usual, the biggest problem in their relationship had little to do with whether or not they had enough in common. The biggest problem was that he crossed an absolute line in her unwritten list of no-nos: he was abusive.

After years of raising her kids on her own, she started dating again, but found herself in one relationship after another. My friend thought she knew herself pretty well, but she kept ending up in dysfunctional relationships with threatening, controlling, or abusive men. These guys all presented well on the surface: nice looking, friendly, fun, smart. But ultimately they had traits that were similar to the **No-No** traits her ex-husband had.

One night I was visiting the home of a friend who was undergoing chemotherapy, and my friend with the boyfriend issues was also visiting. She had brought a new boyfriend along, and this time I noticed something different. At first blush, it would have been easy to dismiss her new guy as the least likely of all the relationship candidates she had dated. He was quiet, while my friend has always been talkative. He did not project excitement, and my friend is lively. And he did not have the kind of looks she usually went for. When he talked about his field, he was well spoken, but she had dated other intelligent men, so that didn't tell me much. Then, as the evening went on, I noticed something about the way he behaved toward everyone in the room.

At one point in the night, our ill friend felt nauseated and was about to throw up. He looked for his wife to help him get up, so he could make it to the bathroom, but she was nowhere in sight. The new boyfriend jumped up, grabbed a kitchen towel, and held it under my sick friend's mouth. My friend was hesitant but the new guy gestured not to worry about it. So our friend more-or-less threw up in the new boyfriend's towel-covered hand. What's more, the new guy cleaned everything up, including our friend, with genuine compassion and calm, waving off his embarrassment.

I was impressed by his simple caring. He was also helpful with serving the food, picking up dishes, and helping people in little unobtrusive ways—not just the date he might have hoped to impress, but everyone. Mind you, this was the first time he had met any of us, and none of us expected him to help out at all.

In later conversations with my friend, I could tell she did not want to choose him, because he did not fit her profile. I reminded her that her complaints about her previous dates were things like: "He was controlling," "He was not very caring," or "He was selfish." I reminded her of her new boyfriend's behavior with our sick friend. With that, I advised her, "What you want is someone caring and unselfish, and his behavior that night was testimony of his genuine caring and unselfishness. I know he doesn't have the physical attributes you usually look for. But if you can get past that first impression, you will see that he's most likely who you want as a partner."

She hesitated. "I don't know." She was already halfway convinced to dismiss him and keep searching, because he did not fulfill the mental list she had of the traits she wanted. But I convinced her that the important thing here was that he was the opposite of the one thing she was sure she did not want. He was not cruel. He was genuinely kind. More importantly, he did not cling to her all night. "Clingy" was definitely on her unwritten, but often spoken, **No-No List**.

She gave it a whirl, and they ended up in a loving marriage. By spending time with a man who fit her unwritten **No-No List,** she came to realize that the things she did not want really had something to say about who she was and what she needed. Along the way, she admitted how right that decision was. "I have a busy life and I like to have my own time with my friends and have plenty of me-time. This guy's not too needy. He understands that I need my space, he helps me with a lot of things, and he's not threatened by my success. In fact, he's very supportive of me. He's even-tempered and calm." She also admitted that she forgot she ever had reservations about him not looking or acting like her type.

My friend had spent years going after what she thought was her type. But she had been wrong. Not because she lacked intelligence, or was unwilling to know herself, or was self-destructive. She had simply made the same honest mistake many people make: she thought that the key to finding Mr. Right was finding someone she was attracted to and had plenty in common with. That was a start. But it was not the key. The key was avoiding what she did not want, and through that discovering what she did want.

What You Don't Want Reveals You

Your **No-No List** helps to define you and your personality. Looking at what you don't want in life draws an outline around what you do want, helping you to learn more about who you are. It is not just the things you don't want, but rather the *words* you use to describe them, that reveal the most. Sure, everybody would like somebody supportive. But when you use the phrase, "I don't want somebody who suffocates me," that is very telling. It suggests that you know what it feels like to be trapped and that you need someone who will not push that button. It tells me that you want to be independent, that freedom is a significant value for you, that you don't want to be tied down or to have to take care of someone else's needs all the time. You might like to be there for someone else, but you don't want to be the one person your partner relies on to do it all. What you want is a real partner who does his or her share.

By the same token, you might say, "I don't want someone who doesn't trust me." Then I know that you have probably suffered through relationships where someone had you on a short leash, when what you clearly value most is your independence. You want a partnership in which both of you express your individuality, a relationship in which the other person is very capable of taking care of himself or herself, and does not expect you to explain all your actions. You are not flattered by someone who constantly asks questions like "Where were you last night? Why didn't you answer the phone?" To you that person is clingy, and you want to be your own person.

Let's say your list also indicates you don't want a "Boaster," someone who spends a lot of time telling you how great he or she is, regularly hauling out a list of achievements. That indicates that you value modesty, humility, and a down-to-earth approach to life. It might mean that you are a modest person yourself, or that you have a strong ego that gets squashed when someone boasts, or maybe that you simply don't like confrontation—and experience has taught you that boasting is a sign of insecurity that could lead to a confrontation.

Your description of what you mean by "Boaster" will help you figure out what it is that's driving that no-no for you. Meanwhile, as you head into the dating scene with your list tucked away at home, and memorized in your head, you will begin to see your motivations in a new light. You will meet someone and look at your list and begin to piece it together: "Ah yes, now I see why that was so important to me: when I'm with a boaster I feel like it's all about them, and there's no room for me," or whatever the revelation is for you.

Your self-knowledge deepens by knowing your **No-No List**. Maybe you thought you knew yourself just fine before, and maybe you did. But knowing who you are and what you need as a single person can be a bit different from knowing who you are and what you need in a long-term partnership. The dynamics shift when we start to seek a life partner versus someone to enjoy an evening with. This is a new kind of self-knowledge that allows you to begin to explore not just who you are, but also what kind of people will help bring out the best in you.

Will the Real You Stand Up?

The **No-No List** will reveal a lot about yourself that you might not have thought much about before, and that kind of self-awareness is not always easy to deal with. There's nothing wrong with sneaking up on this self-knowledge slowly. This process works, but only if you are willing to cut yourself some slack.

If you are not willing to admit to yourself what you don't want, for fear you might be ashamed of what that reveals about you, then you are going to keep getting what you don't want. If you pretend that the behaviors and attitudes you hate don't drive you nuts, then both you and your partner are going to pay the price; you will pay the price for as long as you lie about being happy, and your partner will pay the price as soon as he or she realizes your love is not as it seems. You cannot hide your true self from your partner forever, so best never to start. Remember, the trait that one person believes is your most shallow quality, another person might call practicality. One person might believe the things you don't want make you a flake, while another person might say they only make you a free spirit.

Nobody ever lists on an online dating profile: "I'm a gold digger looking for a rich man." Some people might feel that way, but most know that society will look down on it. But your **No-No List** is private, and if you are looking for financial security with a partner who has a good education, a professional career, and plenty of ambition, what's wrong with that? The thing is, you will only know how deep that desire goes if you can admit, "I don't want to marry a person who is not well off," or "I don't want to marry an uneducated person," or "I don't want to marry a person who lacks ambition." This is not the time to pretend to be open minded about something when you have already made up your mind.

You might fear that people will think you are judgmental if you decide you will not date people with low-paying jobs. Or you might fear that you will limit yourself by not dating those people. But if you fear poverty, it is better to be honest with yourself about that now. If it is important to you to feel financially secure, and you date an uneducated, working-class person who lacks ambition, you are guaranteeing a life full of conflict— for both of you. If you feel bad now for not wanting to date someone who is low on cash, imagine how bad you will feel later when you make that person feel like a failure for not being able to provide you with the things you want. Whatever makes you that person who fears poverty probably runs deep, and is not going to change.

If you like the idea of a man, or a woman, who has money to lavish on you or to help support you, I have good news: there are people out there who would love to do just that for someone who also fulfills *their* needs. If financial stability is important to you, then you should probably learn more about the other person's financial standing before you start dating, or at least before you go on a second date. If someone invites you to a movie and a fast-food joint, and cannot afford to pay, you are doing yourself a disservice if you rationalize: "But he's so sweet, maybe I can learn to deal with living on a budget," or "But she's such a talented artist, maybe she'll get discovered." You are kidding yourself. Let your **No-No List** be your guide back to reality. He won't stay sweet 24/7, and if getting rich were her priority she would have reflected on the meaning of the phrase "starving artist."

Being real about who you are and what you want is a much easier road to being a good guy, or a nice girl.

It is your right to want whatever you want. You just have to be willing to pay the price that goes with having it. The lower the price you are willing to pay, the longer you might have to shop. For example, if your partner is going to pay for you to enjoy an expensive lifestyle, he or she might expect you to fulfill certain obligations in return: be a stay-at-home parent, help with political functions, adhere to an allowance, travel where your spouse travels, or any number of things. Are you willing to go that far?

Then it might be a match made in heaven. Not willing to go that far? You can wait for a better combination or reconsider what you are willing to let go.

The relationship you are looking for is private. It starts as a relationship between **you** and **you**, as you get to know yourself and what matters to you. It continues to be private when it becomes a partnership between you and one other person—and nobody else. So you need not fear the truth about you, or that other person. In fact, you must know the truth about you or no relationship will ever work for you.

If you are honest about what you don't want, and you find someone who is honest about what he or she does not want, then you are going to find someone who will love you as is. The only way you are going to get to that point is if you are willing to first accept yourself as is.

I am not saying we should not seek to grow and change. I am talking about core characteristics. You might shift your behavior a little around those things, but that core will not change. If you can admit that now, you will save yourself a lot of heartache.

The No-No List Never Blames You

Although wisdom sometimes comes with age, that does not mean it grows easier to admit our mistakes. Our brains like us to feel comfortable and secure, and thinking of ourselves as being prone to error makes that difficult. So the brain tends to block out any reasoning that makes us look wrong. Nobody really wants to admit, "I've made terrible mistakes in my relationships." It is painful to consider the idea that we might screw up our own lives. "But it was a great learning experience" is not as comforting as we would like to think. That is another reason the

No-No List is such a great tool. It does not blame you. It does not blame your past partners either.

Nobody wants to be wrong. For better or worse, our society tends to teach us that mistakes are bad, or at least not desirable. In therapy, I try to point out to my clients that the purpose of looking at the mistakes of the past is not about blame, but about accepting their lessons so they can move on to better choices. Even then, clients have a hard time accepting this without feeling either anger at being blamed for something they see as not their fault, or guilt over something they have taken on as all their fault.

Sometimes people choose to go through therapy to deal with the feelings of guilt or blame they have about their relationships. Discovering forgiveness, self-acceptance, and growth on the other side is part of the reward. But this book is not therapy, and neither is the **No-No List**.

The **No-No List** is not a blunt instrument for you to use to beat yourself up, or to beat up anybody else. It is a tool to help guide you in discovering what is best for you, by first eliminating what is worst.

If this chapter has brought you a step closer to true self-acceptance, it's time to go back and look over your **No-No List** once again and see if there are items that you would be wise to add, revise, or remove.

Chapter 9

✗ ✗ ✗ ✓

Put the Real You Out There

Under the Surface

Attraction can lead to true love, but we all know there is much more to it than that, and the **No-No List** will help you dig deeper to find all the other things you truly need. The search for the kind of deep love that leads to long-term commitment has little to do with looks, charm, or a list of perfect qualities. It begins with knowing who you are and being satisfied with all you have to offer. It leads to finding somebody else who gets who you are and is satisfied with all you have to offer. It ends with you being able to honestly do the same for that person.

An overweight man, a bald woman, a wealthy career-woman, a poor man: they can all find a mate, so long as they begin by being who they are.

If you truly want a match, you can find one, no matter what obstacles you think you have to overcome. I often hear overweight people say, "Nobody would want someone fat like me." To these people I say, "It's not about fat, it's about self-confidence." Go to the mall. Sit there for a couple of hours, and observe how many overweight people you see walking with a mate.

The **No-No List** is not a guarantee of finding perfection. It is a guideline to help you avoid wasting time with those people who are most likely to be totally wrong for you. Mr. or Ms. Right will show up only if the true you shows up. Being the true you begins with embracing not only what you want, but also what you don't want. Your **No-No List** is a compass to the true you, a compass that will help guide you away from the wrong mate, and in so doing will help you find the right one.

Keep Looking in Your Favorite Places

People tend to hunt for potential mates in social groups. My clients and friends who have had trouble finding a match have often concluded that they were looking for love in all the wrong places. People often assume the problem must be with the church, the hiking club, the bar, or the dance class they've chosen. If that's what you've been thinking, I can assure you: the problem is not the groups, activities, or places where you spend time. The problem is that, up to now, you did not get to know yourself and come to accept yourself as you are, so you did not know what to look for—or rather, you did not know what to avoid.

If you believe in the teachings of a particular church, if you love to hike, if you find joy in dancing, or if you like the bar scene, then any of those can be the right places for you. If you have a close friend whose company you enjoy, and that person throws parties now and then, I assure you that you can find the right person at one of those parties. There is a reason you visit those places, groups, and friends so often. They reflect some aspect of you. The right person is in one of those places.

Why has your search through your usual stomping grounds turned up nothing so far? You have probably been moving through your groups and focusing on the first person you felt attracted to with whom you shared something in common. Chemistry is important, but you cannot park there. You have to keep going until you find the person with whom you not only feel chemistry, with whom you not only have things in common, but with whom you also hear an absence of alarm bells. What alarm bells? The ones that tell you this person likely has one of those non-negotiable traits that will drive you over the edge in the long run. You are not going to know how to cross-reference those three things—chemistry, common values, and an absence of non-negotiables—unless you do your homework.

Finding someone with whom you
share chemistry and common interests is
a great combo for a whirlwind romance, but
if you do not add rationality to the mix it
may also be a great combo for a
heart-wrenching breakup.

Keep looking for your match among the people, places, and things that interest you. But don't meet someone and then try to force yourself to fit into that person's interests. If you gravitate toward the fair-haired guy who looks fantastic in a suit, and you join his book club even though you hate reading, or you fixate on the girl with the athletic body and join her health club even though you hate working out, you and your chosen mate are headed for heartbreak.

Display Your Warts and All

If you want your **No-No List** to work, you cannot put on a façade for any first date, or for the beginning of any relationship. That is another reason so many people end up with the wrong partner. If they act like someone they are not, they will only attract people who are seeking the kind of person they are not. If you want to find the right person, you have to come to terms with who you are. Until you get okay with you, you are going to be miserable no matter who you end up with, because you cannot keep up the act forever. At some point, your partner will find out that some of his or her habits are no-nos in your book, and at some point, you will have to let your guard down and break some of the no-nos in theirs. When that day comes, the other person is bound to feel deceived and you are bound to feel disappointed.

We know from experience that there are certain things some people do not like about us. Maybe they are the same things we do not like about ourselves. If you are an adult, those things are unlikely to change dramatically. You might learn to adjust your behavior for social situations, but that only goes so far. Regardless of whom you find a relationship with, you will have a relationship with yourself for your entire life. So learn to accept yourself, warts and all.

If you hide your true self, you will never find someone who loves you as you are. You will only succeed in living a lie with a person who loves you for something you are not.

This is a two-way street. If you want to avoid someone who is a no-no for you, you have to accept that you are going to be a no-no for someone else. Being honest is the best way to avoid wasting time. If you are a casual person but you dress in a suit for the first date, you are going to give an erroneous impression. Someone like my friend Brandy would love you, but only until the real you finally shows up one day in jeans and a t-shirt. Not only would she be disappointed, but she would also be angry that you prevented her from meeting a great guy who loves suiting up.

One of the hardest things about living by the **No-No List** is having the courage to walk away from someone you are attracted to because you know that it will not work. Finding the right person sometimes requires having the courage to remain alone if need be, so that you can stay available for the quality relationship you really want. Sometimes you have to remind yourself that you are better off living alone than entertaining false hope.

Being Yourself Does Matter

Times have changed. People did not used to spend much time figuring out who they were, but human awareness has evolved, so relationships must evolve or end up trampled by human progress. Among those of us whose parents were born before the

Women's Movement, very few ever saw our fathers or mothers doing a lot to develop themselves as individuals outside of the family unit. Maybe men would go hunting or bowling, or women would take up sewing . . . or bowling. The idea of a girls' night out was rare until the 1980s. For most of the last century, the closest facsimile to that might have been to go to a neighbor's house for a cup of coffee, or put the baby in a stroller and walk to a park to talk to other moms.

My generation marked the beginning of a new guard. I spent some time working to help put my husband through school, which women have done before. The new change was that my husband also worked to help put *me* through school. That meant that, for a time, he was the primary person taking care of our son and the house, a job that was formerly seen as the province of women. By bending these once-rigid roles, we have both had a chance to grow as individuals in ways we might not have in past eras—my husband's opportunities have expanded as much as mine. I have had a chance to explore a career instead of having a strictly defined role as a stay-at-home mom, while my husband has had a chance to discover what it's like to nurture a child and to have someone help support him instead of bearing the burden of bringing home the bacon alone.

We are still learning to slough off those old roles. The habits of centuries of socialization do not go away overnight. Allow me to affirm that it is not selfish to have individual goals, desires, and dreams, and to want to hold on to those after you are married. You do not have to give up who you are to make another person happy. In fact, if two people can find a way to support each other's individual growth, they can increase each other's happiness. Sharing a life with someone who has real interests and passions in the world can be much more fulfilling than being with someone who simply says, "Whatever you want, dear." When people know the value of investing in their own personal growth, they are more likely to appreciate and nurture that in other people— especially if it means receiving support for their goals in return. This is what makes modern marriage and partnerships so exciting: the opportunity to do more together than we can do apart, not only for each other, but also for ourselves.

There is no contradiction between striving to fulfill yourself and striving to contribute to a family. They go hand-in-hand. The more complete you are as an individual, the more you have to bring to the family table. The trick is that you still need to bring something to the family table. So, for example, if you want to go hunting with your buddies, but the kids need new shoes and the trip is too expensive, you might need to forgo that this year . . . but maybe you can still have a night out with the boys.

What's more, if you do want to do something for yourself, then you have to allow space for your partner to do the same. So the wife wants a night out to do dinner and drinks with the girls, leaving Dad home alone with four kids? Great. But that would be pretty unfair if he could not have his poker night with the boys. Of course, these stories change if she has a drinking problem or he has a gambling addiction, but you get the idea.

Developing yourself goes beyond the idea of nurturing friendships and outside relationships, to becoming the most you can be. I initially became a dentist because it was a practical and challenging profession, and I was happy in my career for years. After being forced to retire from dentistry due to a shoulder injury, my lifetime passion for helping people led me to change my career to counseling. This meant more time in school at a time in life when many couples are saving for retirement. But my husband understood that when I am fulfilled I bring more to the relationship, and we both knew that loving each other has always meant supporting each other's goals. So he took on a few more duties at home while I returned to school. We have traded that role back and forth over the years, and thanks to that we are closer as a couple and happier as individuals. We could not have done as much without each other's support.

If you want to develop as a person, getting to know yourself is part of the bargain. When you develop yourself in tandem with another person, then it is important to know more about who you are in relation to other people. Much of this sort of knowledge starts with knowing what you don't want—for example, knowing that you don't want someone who does not value education. If I had married a man like that, I would not have been able to pursue my dreams.

Remember, the overlapping areas between your life and another person's will never cover the whole relationship. That is not a bad thing. What is the fun in marrying your clone?

Where is the dynamic possibility for new ideas and growth if we are all so alike that we never challenge each other, or reveal to each other anything new?

The attraction might be in the 31 percent we have in common, but it is in that other 69 percent that we can embark on a voyage of mutual discovery. That is where we can surprise ourselves into trying something new: a new kind of food or sport or book, a new way of keeping house or planning a business, a new way of seeing social policy or community. We might find ourselves supporting our partner in things we would never consider for ourselves: becoming a triathlete, opening an ice cream shop, going back to school, volunteering for a political committee.

Why are we willing to do these things? Partly because we love someone else and want to support her or him, but partly because when we support someone else we discover and create new parts of ourselves. That is not just a way of loving others; that is a way to love ourselves.

Your Partner Needs to Know Your No-Nos

It is not enough to simply know your no-nos. You have to be willing to let any potential partner in on what you value, and the things you don't want are an important part of that. Trust me, it is a lot easier to let someone in on the true you up front, rather than go through the expensive embarrassment of a messy breakup or divorce later. However, I will admit that these revelations go on throughout the entire relationship as people evolve and grow.

Somewhere along the way, my husband had heard that women need to be complimented all the time. So one morning he tried out this theory. The moment he woke up and saw me getting ready for my day, he let his eyes open wide with a look that suggested he had never seen anyone so beautiful before.

Then he said something like, "Oh my God, that color looks so good on you!"

I was so surprised I almost burst out laughing. Then I quickly stepped into my closet so he could not see me, stuck my head out, and quizzed him, "Okay, what color am I wearing, honey?"

He was caught. "I don't know. Whatever you're wearing . . . it just looks nice."

I stepped out of the closet and said, "I don't need you to flatter me. I don't like that sort of thing. I just want you to be truthful."

"I just want you to know I love you," he said.

"I do know that. I can read between the lines of all the things you do. You don't need to give me compliments just for their own sake."

It's not that I don't like my husband telling me I'm beautiful now and then. But if he does it all the time it becomes meaning-less. I needed him to know that if he were to make it a practice, it might strike me as insincere, and that his sincerity is more important to me. I shared one of my no-nos, and he was glad to hear it. He really did want to let me know he loved me and I let him know that he was already expressing it in better ways. He was happy to receive the information.

What I told my husband might not be true for all women. Some might like extra attention from their husbands, and some husbands might feel sincerely moved to say such things every day. But by telling him my no-no, I was expressing my own par-ticular value in my own particular way.

Balancing Your Needs With Someone Else's

When you list your no-nos, you need to respect that the person you are looking for is going to have a **No-No List** too. As your no-nos teach you who you are, they also teach you how to look for signs that reveal who the other person is. Often what you discover with no-nos is that it is only a no-no if it creates a situation in which you are not finding a harmony between your needs and your partner's needs.

Personally, I need an hour of quiet time every night. I real-ize this is not something all people need, but it is critical to my sense of inner equilibrium and peace. For that hour of quiet time, I don't want to talk to anybody, I don't want to hear any-body, I don't want to entertain anybody. Most of all, I don't want to have to explain or defend whatever I'm doing during that quiet time. If I am doing a yoga pose, or sitting in my office staring into space, or drinking tea and doodling on a pad, then during my quiet time that is my business and nobody else's.

I will tell you that usually what I am doing during that time is simply processing my day, thinking about what I did well, what I did not do well, what I learned from it all, where it all will take me next. This is important to me because my days are so busy and full of noise that I often do not have time to stop and understand what it all means, and also because I simply need time to decompress and become calm. My quiet time helps me rest and renew myself as I prepare to go to sleep for the night and then start a new day.

Earlier in my marriage, my husband did not understand my need for quiet time. When I suddenly checked out after whirling around all day, he worried that it must mean something about him. "Why don't you want me around?" "I'm your friend and we talk about everything. Why don't you want to talk to me about what's on your mind?" "Did I say something wrong?"

It drove me a little nuts, but I tried to see it from his point of view and allay his concerns: "Honey, I love talking to you, but at that time of night I need to just shut down. As long as I'm telling you about my problems of the day, I'm still venting. I cannot shut down. I need to wind down before I can go to bed."

There was a potential conflict there, because he did not understand my need for quiet time and took it personally. One of *his* no-nos is "Lack of transparency." He does not like having to read between the lines. Meanwhile, I worried he was becoming needy. "Needy" is one of the items on my personal **No-No List**. Luckily, we talked about it. I found out that he was not needy and that the situation was not transparent enough to him. I had not needed "quiet time" when we first married and he was thrown off by the change. I explained that when we were younger I did not feel the weight of as many responsibilities, so I did not need that one hour of quiet time. Something in the relationship had changed and he simply needed to understand what it was.

We both had encountered a no-no that we did not know the other person had brought to the relationship. But once we brought it out in the open and discussed it, we were able to find a way to balance each other's individual needs.

These surprises will come up throughout any relationship, but if you do not discuss such issues at the beginning, you potentially saddle yourself with an ever-growing list of no-nos that will not yield to compromise. So it is important from the moment you meet a potential partner to be honest about your needs, and to expect the other person to be honest about his or hers. Then you can begin the process of discovering whether it is possible to strike a balance between them, or whether you have hit a no-no that is really a "No Way."

Learning the Right Reasons to Say No

Any person can make small shifts in activities, habits, and communication style to accommodate others. In a world of seven billion people that's a necessity for survival. But nobody's fundamental character and personality ever change, except maybe with traumatic brain injury. If people did change like that, they would cease to be themselves. What is the point of a change so drastic you are no longer yourself? You would cease to exist. Your home, the place where you spend the majority of your time, is the place where you are least likely to feel motivated to change your very nature. That would be asking for phoniness at an exhausting level.

You are going to spend *a lot* of time at home with your life partner. If you try to keep up a façade in this most intimate part of your life, you'll find it an impossible task. You will eventually become resentful and your partner will feel deceived. It is much easier to be honest from the get-go, so that you can make sure to find someone who can handle that.

Most people are not "made for each other." Even couples who have plenty in common will inevitably find that 69 percent of their lives is divergent. Couples who are not well suited tend to each have traits that drive the other person mad, often for very good reasons. That does not mean either of them is inept, inadequate, or immoral. Usually they simply have different sets of values, needs, or approaches.

Even when we come from the same culture, there are many microcultures we all come from, many tribes, all the way down to the tribes within individual homes. Each of those tribes has its own worldview. We do nobody any favors when we try to make someone from another tribe subscribe to our worldview, or when we subscribe to someone else's worldview by changing ourselves or pretending to be someone different. Instead, if we want to find compatible companionship, we must find our true selves and then our true tribe.

Early on in my marriage, I had to face my husband's 69 percent. Like many young people, I tried very hard to change him, with little to no result. Once I let go of trying to make my husband more interested in going out dancing and socializing or pursuing some grand purpose, I realized that what I had thought of as boring and unambitious was simply a different set of interests and ambitions. He did not need to make a splash in his career, but he did have the ambition of creating a harmonious family. That was something I could support because family was a big value for me. I could support him in being the best of who he was. The surprising gift was that this was not only good for him; it also provided a balance to my go-getter lifestyle. He became my rock, I became his wings. Sometimes we even traded places. If I had spent my life trying to make him like me, our relationship would have headed straight for a train wreck.

Of course, you cannot plan for everything in marriage. Maybe you marry someone who has a couple of glasses of wine with dinner, which you enjoy too. No problem. But maybe after ten or twenty years of marriage, your partner hits a bump in the road that sends him or her deeper and deeper into drinking to escape problems. One day you realize that, even though you did not marry a drunk, you have ended up married to one anyway. The question will have to be answered: Is this a no-no I can live with and accommodate, or is it an absolute no-no and do I have to leave the relationship?

The No-No List cannot cover all future possibilities. That is no reason to avoid looking at the ones you can. In fact, it is all the more reason to minimize those potentials now.

The **No-No List** is not about learning to say "No" to every little thing that bothers you. If you did that, you would never find a mate at all. It is about rationally looking at all the cards in your hand, not just the ones that you think can win you the game, but also the ones that are not helping you at all. You are deciding based on having all the information in front of you, not just part of it. You are learning to rationally decide if this is a good bet, not just for now, but for a long time to come. You cannot make that gamble based only on what about this hand of cards makes you happy. You have to look at all the things about this person that make you unhappy and decide whether you can embrace those things too.

If you are going to say "Yes" to someone, it has to include everything about that person. If you are going to say "No," make sure it is for the right reasons. This cannot be just because the way he picks his teeth after dinner drives you nuts, but rather because he has obsessive-compulsive disorder and you are not up for that huge a challenge.

If you had to play this one hand for the rest of your life, would you mind carrying around those extra cards? The point is that when it comes to your partner, he brings one set of cards to the table and one set only. So you cannot just pick and choose which cards to keep and which to discard. Remember, these cards often change depending on who is holding them. What looks like a bad hand to you might look like a royal flush to someone else. Why hang on to it, hoping it will turn into a royal flush for you, when there is already someone out there who can see it that way?

Be the **true you**, and when you meet your **true other,** you will finally see how even the bad cards can become your own royal flush. Will the true you now pull out the **No-No List** once again and make sure it reflects you just as you are?

Chapter 10

X X X ✔

The Value of Self-Acceptance

Self-Acceptance Makes Growth and Change Possible

Sometimes no-nos do evolve, change, or go away, but only because *you* change. You can never change another person. You can only change yourself. Do not let it worry you if you cannot change things about yourself that you believe need changing, or if you do not want to change things about yourself that others believe you should. There truly is someone out there who will accept you as you are. Here's the catch: before that can happen, you first must accept yourself, with all your unique quirks, habits, and imperfections. If you do not, people will never see you as you really are, and you will continue to attract people who only want you for those things you are pretending to be.

If you do not first accept yourself, the
No-No List cannot help you.

I am not suggesting that you stop growing. On the contrary, the simple step of being honest about who you are represents tremendous growth. It also creates a strong foundation for continued growth. Now that you accept who you are, you can begin leaning into your strengths and finding the ways in which some of the things you thought were weaknesses might actually be turned into strengths. As you become aware of your less user-friendly qualities, you can find outlets for them that do not negatively impact others.

The more success you have at being yourself, the more confidence you will have. That confidence may cause you to redirect some of those qualities that used to get you into trouble. Some of them might even fade away, because many of the bad habits we rely on to interact with others are based on insecurity. As you put your true self out there and discover those people who have a use for the real you, you will lose many of the insecurities that might have caused you to behave in unnatural or unhealthy ways.

You Can't Please Everyone

You will always have a mix of qualities that some people like and some people don't. This is true of all of us. When we accept the fact that we cannot please everyone no matter what we do, we begin to find that it is much less exhausting to simply be ourselves. As we do that, we discover people who are okay with us even when we make mistakes.

People who share your values will believe in you. They will see the relationship with you as an investment. You each might have to put a lot into it, and sometimes you each might take a lot out of it, but in the end you will both see a benefit. Such are the gifts of finding your tribe, the people who share your worldview and approach to life.

As you learn to respect yourself and what you have to offer, you will begin to offer more of it. Those who are grateful for your gifts will return the favor by offering gifts of their own to your life. This is true of any relationship: marriage, friendship, business partnership, employer-employee, customer-seller, client-contractor, project collaborators, supportive neighbors, and more. When you offer the real you, people who appreciate that will offer the same in return. This creates bonds of affection, interdependence, mutual support, mentorship, sacrifice, and more, which benefit both parties.

If being true to yourself reaps so many rewards, then it only makes sense to offer any potential partners the same respect: to expect them to be no more and no less than their true selves. Sometimes this may mean that you learn things about other people that you do not like. That is not something that should scare you, but should instead make you grateful. Because they have been honest about those things, you now both have an opportunity to choose whether this truly is the right partnership for you, or whether you both need to seek other more suitable partnerships that will better serve your interests, needs, and values.

Wouldn't you prefer if somebody put up a sign that said, "Caution: hazardous materials ahead. Stay clear," rather than letting you walk into a toxic site without warning? Then why get angry when people reveal who they are through what they do and say?

It is never your place to improve or fix anyone else, any more than it is your job to clean up every toxic waste site you run across. Sure, if it is a problem for enough people, you all might consider confronting the person as a group and asking him or her to clean things up. But even then, the solution is not up to you. If you meet otherwise smart, charming, interesting people with emotional problems or mental health issues, you cannot save or fix them. Let them take it up with a therapist or support group.

This goes both ways; even if you come to the table with baggage, it is not up to your partner to unpack it for you.

Sure, some people would benefit from changing things about themselves: alcoholics, for example, would probably be better off if they stopped drinking. But they are just not going to do it unless the impetus comes from within. It is a simple truth of human nature that the more you try to pressure or manipulate people to get them to change, the more they will push back. This is because they see you as a threat to their survival as individuals. If they cannot be themselves, who would they be? Expecting them to be happy that you are trying to improve them is like expecting someone to be happy if aliens landed and decided to replace any humans they did not approve of with improved copies. When you try to change other people, you are essentially asking them to kill the part of themselves that you do not like and replace it with someone else.

It does not matter if the people you want to change really would be better if they changed, even if you only want them to change one or two things about themselves. To some extent, we might all improve in some way if we made minor changes. But in a society with democratic values, we all want that to be up to us as individuals, nobody else. Letting others impose their values and interests on us, no matter how good those values and interests might be, is something no independent person will easily bear.

Who Are You, Really?

In relationships, perhaps the worst tyranny of all is the one we inflict on ourselves when we give in to the real or perceived expectations of others that we must change to suit them. In fact, this is not something others can easily do to us unless we first do it to ourselves. It is natural to want to belong, to be part of a group, to participate in society. So of course we find ways to cooperate, to maximize whatever might smooth the way socially, and to minimize whatever might make social interaction bumpy. Still, we often overestimate what it might take to do that.

> Finding love and belonging does require give and take. But it should never require us to become so unlike ourselves that we can barely recognize who we are.

Consider how far Jana went to reshape herself to the needs of others, and the heartbreaking results:

I met Jana and her husband Cliff when they came to me for therapy. Jana and Cliff had worked together before they dated and subsequently married. When I met them they had been married for four years and had two kids. They came to therapy to address Cliff's infidelity.

Back when Jana and Cliff worked together, she knew that Cliff had a reputation as a ladies' man and that he had dated a few coworkers. She thought she could hold Cliff's attention by becoming everything he wanted in a woman. She lost weight, changed her hair color to blonde, acted more adventurous, and took care of Cliff like his mother would.

After they married and had their first baby, one night Jana woke up and noticed Cliff was not in bed with her. He often stayed up late working, so she decided to go downstairs to give him a kiss and thank him for working so hard for the family. Cliff had fallen asleep in front of his computer, but what she saw on the screen shocked her. He was engaged in a romantic online chat with a woman from work. Over the next couple of weeks, she found out that he had been chatting like that with several women, as well as meeting them at various hotels to have sex. When she confronted him, he apologized, swore he loved her, and explained that he had felt lonely because Jana was so focused on the baby and needed to refrain from sex after a Caesarian section. He swore it would not happen again.

When it did happen again, they came to me. Jana said she did not understand why Cliff cheated again since she had gone out of her way to make sure he was not neglected. She had hired a nanny to take care of the kids a few nights a week so she could spend time with Cliff, she had gone with him on business trips to keep him company, and she had catered to his desire for sexual variety and fantasy. One night she had dressed in a maid's outfit, and another night they had pretended to meet like strangers in a bar and have a one-night stand. She admitted it was not her style: "I did not like myself while I was doing those things and I was very unhappy."

Therapy could not save Jana's marriage. This was not about whether she was doing enough to please her husband, it was about what each of them truly did and did not want in a relationship. Cliff did not want a commitment, but preferred variety and the thrill of the chase. Meanwhile, Jana did not want a man who could not commit and who lied about it.

When I delved into Jana's history I found out that she had been in three other committed relationships before marrying Cliff. In her first relationship, she had stopped putting on makeup, doing her hair, or wearing nice clothes because her boyfriend liked natural-looking women. Then she started budget backpacking in undeveloped countries because he wanted someone more adventurous. She missed looking pretty and hated staying in hostels.

Her second relationship was with a man from an affluent family. For him, she went to the other extreme, dressing in uncomfortable designer clothes and attending charity balls. She said that made her feel phony and out of place.

Her third relationship was with a man ten years her junior. She was thirty-two and he was twenty-two. She partied four to five days a week, drinking and dancing until she dropped. She found it exhausting and sophomoric, but she felt that acting like a college student was necessary to keep her man.

All the men in Jana's life loved aspects of her, and she loved aspects of them, but the acceptance was never complete. She constantly changed parts of herself to suit them, but she could only become somebody else for so long. She attributed her failed relationships to not having enough in common. This was true, but it always took a long time to figure that out because she pretended to have things in common. Therapy helped her to see that she needed to know herself first before committing to a relationship.

To have a healthy relationship with others, you must first have a healthy relationship with yourself. To that end, it can help to ask the same questions about yourself that I have suggested you ask about others. If you want to learn who you are, begin by asking: *who am I not?* If you want to understand what you want from a relationship with yourself, begin by asking: *what is it I do not want from this relationship?*

Maybe those qualities about yourself that you do not like really are something that would be worth changing. Welcome to the club. That is, the club of humanity. If we were all already perfect, had everything we needed, and had already become everything we wanted to be, where would the adventure be? One of the benefits of throwing ourselves into the passions and pursuits that interest us is that they create opportunities for us to grow.

That does not mean that you are not fantastic as you are, or that you should wait until you grow before going out there and finding the right person. Romance and marriage are part of life's many opportunities for growth.

Someone Who Supports Your Personal Growth

Nobody should have to become perfect before they find someone. The challenge is finding the perfect partner to grow with, someone who accepts you as you are but who also sees your potential. I do not mean the kind of potential that requires you to change in the ways someone else thinks best. I mean you want to find someone who sees your potential and believes in your ability to achieve it in your own way.

Might the right partner offer you suggestions for growth and change? Might he or she challenge you? Might he or she grow angry with you if you change in ways that cause discomfort in the relationship? Of course. But the right partner will never make you feel that you owe it to them to become someone different. Only you know where that line is. The wrong person will cross that line fairly early on. Like you, other people are looking for the signs: is this a person who is okay with me pushing or pulling in this direction? Is this someone who will support the direction I want to go? Is this someone whose direction I can support? You do nobody any favors by hiding or burying your warning signs, by hiding or burying the truth.

Growth is good, and around the
right person it will happen.

If a plant receives sun, water, and nourishment from the soil, it will grow well, but it will still only grow in the direction that best suits it, to the height that best suits it, displaying the fruits that best suit it. Requiring a particular change from yourself or from another is not going to help you find love, receive love, or give love.

Where Self-Love and Loving Others Overlap

The old adage that you cannot love another until you love yourself has much deeper implications than its simplicity initially reveals. What does it mean to love yourself? Does a narcissist love himself? Clearly not enough. If he did, he would feel much too complete and satisfied within to insist on so much attention from others. When we truly love ourselves, we want to share the best of ourselves with others. On the other hand, does a person with a caretaking personality love herself for her generosity? Maybe, or maybe she is just afraid that other people will not love her unless she is useful to them. When we love ourselves, we find ways to meet our own needs so that we have the energy to help others meet theirs. It is all a matter of balance.

How do we balance loving ourselves with loving others? The answer is unique for each relationship, just as we are all unique. There are billions of individuals on this planet, and each and every one has been shaped by unique life experiences. Among those billions, you will always find people whose values and interests overlap with yours, but you will never find someone whose values and interests overlap with yours in *every way*.

If you want a lasting relationship, then you are looking for someone who will offer acceptance and understanding in those areas of your lives where there is no overlap.

I have told you a lot of stories about wrong turns in the search for love, but here's one about a guy who made all the right moves to find a relationship filled with acceptance and understanding. Max was a fifty-five-year-old banker who lost his wife in a car accident. At the time, he had a twelve-year-old daughter and an eight-year-old son. He found himself approached by many interested women, but he took his time. *He knew what he did not want.* Most importantly: he did not want to marry a woman his kids would not accept. His standards for a mate revolved around his kids, who were his first priority; he wanted someone caring, who loved children, who understood that his primary responsibility was to his daughter and son.

Many women Max met acted as if they were into kids, but before he agreed to date any of them he checked them against his own mental **No-No List,** asked them their stories, and observed them over a long period of time in many social situations. Their behavior often told him that although they might like children, they did not have what it took to put his children before any other consideration. A few of them were divorced and shared backstories in which it was clear that they had involved their children in their disagreements with their exes. Max knew those were red flags.

Then Max met Danielle, a fifty-four-year-old woman with a thriving business who had never been married. When Danielle shared her personal history, it meant a lot to Max to know that she had lost her mother to cancer at age twelve and had been raised by a loving stepmother of whom she always spoke highly. Danielle was honest about how she felt about kids: she loved children, but did not want to marry someone with very small children, younger than school-age, because she did not believe she could handle that responsibility while maintaining her demanding business.

Max told her that his daughter had a hard time with the idea of replacing her mother. Danielle understood that sentiment from her own experience, and she agreed with Max to put off meeting the children for the first two years they dated. She also agreed with Max's wisdom of gradually drawing her into his family life.

At first, Danielle only participated in a few family functions. She was such a caring person that even the parents of Max's late wife, who were very involved with their grandchildren, suggested that Max should marry Danielle.

Max's daughter loved Danielle, but still resisted the idea of Danielle marrying her dad. So although Danielle was treated like family, she and Max waited until his daughter went to college before marrying. Even then, Danielle did not sell her own home for the first two years after the wedding, just in case the adjustment to a stepmother became too much for Max's son.

I have asked Danielle if it ever bothers her that she comes in third in Max's life. She said, "Absolutely not. Max and I know we'll be together forever, but we both want what's best for the kids." What's more, she said, "If Max did not make the kids his priority, I would not have even considered dating him, let alone marrying him. That would have told me that he was not a caring person and did not take his responsibilities seriously." In her mind, if someone did not show great care for his children, that would be a red flag that he would not be caring toward her.

Max and Danielle both knew not only what they did want, but also what they did *not* want. They knew and accepted themselves and what they were willing to sacrifice. They understood that sacrifice was necessary to a good relationship, because each person brings huge aspects of their lives that are unique to them into a marriage.

Good Trait/Bad Trait

Whether we see our own character traits as positive or negative can be highly subjective. The way we view our own behavior often greatly reflects childhood conditioning. Beyond that, it often depends on the circumstances in which these behaviors arise. So long as you are not living completely outside society's laws or moral codes—engaging in extreme behaviors like violence, fraud, theft, serial adultery, and the like—most other traits can be positive or negative depending on degree or application.

If childhood trauma has conditioned you to view much of your socially acceptable behavior as bad, you might benefit from therapy, a support group, or at least plenty of self-reflection.

However, at some point most of us will have to figure out on our own how to accept the parts of ourselves that we have learned to reject based on conditioning, trauma, or habit.

For example, you might find that people tend to become annoyed with you because you are stubborn, always insistent on doing things your way. This can be a problem in working with other people at times when cooperation is important. However, it can also be indicative of such positive qualities as determination and an unwillingness to give up a goal, which can be positive. It may just be a matter of channeling your stubbornness, knowing when it is serving you and when it is not. Maybe that trait does not serve you in team projects, so maybe you are better off typically working alone. Or you might be a great leader, someone who knows how to make a decision and stick to it, but then you will have to find people who are willing to follow.

The point is, you do not need to give up being a stubborn person to make yourself a desirable partner. There are those who will value your decisiveness and persistence enough that they can be flexible in accepting your stubborn side. In return, perhaps you will find ways to be more flexible. Keep in mind, the people you partner with in life will also bring their own double-edged swords to the table. The more you are willing to seek what is positive in their challenging qualities, the stronger your partnerships will grow.

Even if many people have told you that you act too much this way or not enough that way, that does not mean you have to change. Someone out there won't care, or might even like it.

Even if you have been told by many partners that there is something wrong with you, that does not mean it is true. With most of my clients, I find that the problem is not that one partner or the other has to change.

The Three Most Common Problems in Romantic Partnerships:

1. One or both partners need to stop trying to change the other.
2. One or both partners need to stop trying to change themselves to suit the other.
3. Each partner needs to either find a way to accept the other as is or let that person go and find someone who will.

You can avoid all three of the above problems by promising yourself that you will never ever do these three **No-Nos**:

Three **No-Nos** for Everyone Seeking a Relationship:

1. Never pursue a potential partner who you believe needs to change.
2. Never pursue a potential partner who suggests you should change or for whom you believe you may have to change.
3. Never seek people whom you cannot accept as they are, or who cannot accept you as you are.

Being who you are and expressing that in the world is not easy. It is not as easy to get to know ourselves as we might like to think. We must treat it as any other growing relationship, with respect, honesty, and openness to discovery. We must practice self-awareness as we examine our decisions: Am I choosing this because it is truly an expression of who I am, what I am passionate about, and what I value? Or am I choosing this because

I think I am supposed to, or I have to, or someone else told me to? The answers are not easy. Becoming your truest self is the job of a lifetime.

This is a good time to go back to your **No-No List** and make sure that none of the items on your list are based on pretense, on you trying to turn yourself into someone you're not.

Chapter 11

X X X ✓

When No-No
Means Never-Ever

When Chemistry Fades,
No-Nos Multiply

Some no-nos are deal breakers. When chemistry fades, long-term values become more important. No-nos triggered by our core values become more problematic as time goes on.

When you first get excited about somebody new, your insides likely turn warm and achy and fizzy from a blast of fabulous chemistry. Some of that is physical, and some of it may also be composed of the optimistic belief that this person is exactly right for you. Even when the excitement is greater than anything you have ever before felt for another person, this love-at-first-sight feeling, or even love at second or third sight, does not always equal happily ever after.

As time passes, maybe months, maybe years, you still might be attracted to the other person, you still might do all the things meant to keep romance alive—date nights, surprise outings, holding hands on long walks, making sure to make love—but the biological changes that overtake your body when you first fall in love will level out. No matter how great your relationship, that heart-melting sensation will not stay for the duration.

The first adrenaline rush of romance always fades. I advise people to keep that in mind before they look for love, so they can focus on the qualities that last—for better or worse.

When the initial excitement dies down, that is when the problems become more obvious, even in the best relationships. That is when people often realize, "We don't have this in common," or "I should have looked at that more closely," or "We should have worked out that other issue before." If such problems grow bad enough, it's not unusual to think, "If only I had made a list of what to avoid, I would never have gotten myself into this."

Why We Bother

Marriage can be a rewarding partnership in which two people support each other's goals and dreams, but the day-to-day realities of marriage are not exciting in and of themselves. Marriage can be downright boring at times. When people say you have to work at it, they mean just that. You can keep it from growing boring, but you have to fuel it. After thirty years of being together, if you are not careful you might get so used to each other that you barely notice one another. If you are not proactive about it, sex can take a backseat. You know everything about each other, so the exciting all-night conversations are just not necessary anymore.

My husband and I were driving one day and passed a shop that I like.

He said, "Don't even think about it," and started laughing.

"What are you talking about?" I asked.

"I know you like shopping at that store, and we are not doing it today."

"Oh my God, you can read my mind," I said.

We both shared a good laugh.

Conversations like that are not uncommon for us because we have been together for so long that we have started to learn the way each other's minds work. On one hand, it is endearing. On the other hand, it is not as interesting as those early days of romantic discovery. There is no guessing, no intrigue, no pursuit, no discovery, no mystery anymore. This is not all bad news. Once those things are out of the way, they make room for many other beauties of marriage that come into the picture . . . if you can get that far.

When I first fell in love with my husband, I felt the heart-throb, the butterflies in my stomach, all that. Those sensations may be gone, but now I love him even more than the day I fell for him. We share an unspoken connection, support, stability, mutual reliance, and meeting of minds. He is always there for me. We share the same values. He is my closest friend. We can talk about anything.

I most fully realized how central his support was to my life when my brother passed away. Since my husband was as close to my brother as I was, I felt less inclined to lean on him in my grief because I knew he was feeling weak with grief too. For once, my best friend was not my pillar of strength when I was down. Although that absence made things difficult at the time, it also made me appreciate even more all the times he has been there for me to lean on. In the end, at least we both had someone who understood better than anyone else on earth what the other was going through. There was some relief in that, in not having to explain myself or why I was falling apart. There is a beauty in sharing so intimately with another person.

What will you be left with when the chemistry fades? With a No-No List, you can begin to answer that question.

Romance's initial impulsive chemistry is exciting, but if you want a successful partnership, you must consider people in terms of the aftermath, the years beyond that initial flush of love. In my case, I had a short, mental **No-No List**, less adequate than what I'm offering you—but I got lucky. Since I have been lucky in marriage, I have learned first-hand how letting go of some no-nos can work, but I have also learned why marrying someone who hits all of my no-nos would *never* have worked. The no-nos in my marriage are not deal breakers. This has allowed me some insight into the wisdom of avoiding those deal breakers.

Even my husband and I would have saved ourselves many problems with a couple of **No-No Lists**. If I had gone in with my eyes open to some of his no-nos, I could have practiced more acceptance, cooperation, and planning. If I had done that, we would have avoided a lot of arguments. For example, if I'd had a **No-No List**, I probably would have known earlier that procrastination is a hot button for me. Then I could have spent some time figuring out how to respect that side of him and how to make a plan that would have helped me deal with it.

If you have an effective **No-No List,** it is not about sitting in judgment of a potential partner. Rather, it is about empowering yourself with knowledge that can help you pick a romance that will continue to blossom in new ways instead of wilting after one season.

Mismatched Values are a No-No

Although you fill your **No-No List** with behaviors and personality traits, your decisions will come down to values. What do you value so much that you are unwilling to compromise on it? What behaviors, attitudes, and quirks symbolize a departure from your values?

For me, compassion is a crucial value in a partner, but many other people might say the same. Because of their core character, upbringing, and culture, everyone will express the value of compassion in different ways. Those differences will drive their no-nos. While one person might believe it shows a lack of compassion to refuse financial assistance to the poor, another might believe it shows a lack of compassion to give handouts to the poor and reduce their self-sufficiency. Both people believe in compassion, but they probably would not get along.

I value tolerance for a wide variety of lifestyles, so "Intolerance" would definitely show up on my **No-No List.** However, someone else who values tolerance might put a higher value on adherence to social custom and tradition. To that person, someone who rejects people for not living in accordance with important beliefs is not intolerant, but is simply exercising boundaries. Maybe a different no-no would go on that person's **No-No List,** such as: "Too compromising."

It is in the specifics of the **No-No List**
that you will most easily discover the value
differences between you and others.

Getting Stuck with a No-No Mate

I'll never forget one couple I counseled, perhaps the scariest cautionary tale for what can happen to you if you fail to identify what you don't want. Stephanie and Mike could have avoided a miserable marriage if only they had identified their own no-nos, which were more like never-evers. Stephanie and Mike used to live in another part of the country. Back then, Mike had a great job and they were happy. Stephanie came from a comfortable, upper-middle-class upbringing. Mike had been raised in poverty by a single mom who worked three jobs after his abusive father abandoned the family.

Mike was close to his mother, so when she was diagnosed with a life-threatening illness he was distraught. His mother had no insurance, and although he made good money it was not enough to pay for her treatment. At his job, he had access to money and, like many embezzlers, he told himself he would merely borrow the money to save his mother and then put it back later.

He got caught, and the police arrested him. The company owner felt compassion for Mike's predicament and did not press charges, but the arrest or some aspect of the story remained public record. Mike lost his job, had to move away, and was unable to land such a great position again. Stephanie, who had never known deprivation and could not understand her husband's poor choice, would not forget or forgive what he did, which had changed their lives forever.

By the time I saw them, ten years had passed, but the story came up in our sessions. Stephanie complained about how Mike's poor judgment had ruined their lives. He said he was sorry for what he had done, that he was not a crook by nature but had made a poor decision goaded by concern for his mother. "I couldn't see my mother not getting the necessary treatment. She was in so much pain and I couldn't help her and that pushed me to make the wrong choice."

After I listened to both sides, I told Stephanie, "You need to make a decision. What is it you're here for? Do you want to keep your marriage working?"

"Yes," Stephanie said, looking distressed. "I don't want to get divorced."

"In order to make this relationship work, you need to start thinking, 'What is it about this relationship that I want to change?'"

"The fact that he made such a huge mistake still bothers me."

I said, "It seems to me this was a one-time deal. Did he ever steal before or after that incident? Has he ever been in trouble before?"

"No."

"Okay. I'm not justifying what Mike did, but in this case, it seems like it was a single lapse in judgment while under stress, not a pattern of behavior. So now if you want to stay with him, you're going to have to really put this behind you. You cannot change the past, and you're not going to help your marriage if you keep nagging him about it every day."

I would like to point out that even if she could go back in time, this was not a situation Stephanie could have avoided

by putting "Embezzler" on a **No-No List**. It was not his typi-
cal behavior, and she had no way to guess this might happen.
If, on the other hand, Mike had had a history of legal troubles
before she met him, that might have belonged on the theoret-
ical **No-No List** she made on her trip back in time. If she had
accepted him then, she would be like one of those Mafia wives
who look the other way and become complicit in an illegal life-
style. Rationalizing a no-no can doom you to living a lie. This
wasn't that.

It turned out that the question of him being a crook or not
was not the issue. This was about money and class. I discov-
ered the truth by following another line of questioning: "How
would Mike look if he had all the qualities you wanted? Define
that Mike for me." That is when Stephanie described her well-
to-do family of origin. Her sisters had big houses, nice cars,
expensive vacations, and many comforts. Mike used to give her
those things back when he had a great job. But when they
moved, he could not get a similar position again because of his
record. Now he was working three jobs and they could barely
make ends meet.

Now we were talking! It was not his crime that bothered
her; it was that he could no longer provide for her at the level
she wanted. Once I recognized that, I pursued a different line of
questions: "Tell me how much you think that's going to change.
What else can he do? He works from 8:00 a.m. to 6:00 p.m.
Then he comes home and does odd jobs for the whole neighbor-
hood until 10:00 p.m. Then he works a third job on weekends.
With all that, you're still barely making ends meet, yet you com-
plain that he doesn't spend enough time with you or the kids.
So how would you see that change?" I pointed out that she had
two choices: stay with him, knowing their lifestyle would not
change, or get out of the relationship.

Meanwhile, all Mike wanted was for the nagging to stop.

She was still trying to blame him, saying it was all because of his wrongdoing, but really it was about "I want a lifestyle that's no longer attainable." She wanted a housekeeper like her sisters had. Instead she had to constantly take care of the kids, cook, and clean. She resented her husband, so found reasons to pick on him. She said he never helped around the house.

One of their typical arguments went something like this:

Stephanie said, "I cooked. Why can't you wash dishes? It's been two hours and they're still in the sink."

Mike replied, "I've been up since six this morning, fixed the kids' lunch, took them to school, went to work, came back, worked for the neighbors outside in the heat until ten at night. I haven't even showered yet, and you're asking me why didn't I wash the dishes? They're still sitting in the sink because I was working."

When I asked him what he would like Stephanie to look like in his picture of a life that worked, he replied, "I want somebody caring. I want somebody to understand I'm doing my best. I want her to say, 'You know what? We don't need two luxury cars, look at all we do have!'"

They both decided to stick together because they were Catholic. "We have to stay together," they said. Still, I do not have much hope for the pair. Neither will change. He cannot provide more than he is providing, and he will never be happy with the nagging. She cannot let go of her desire for a higher-class lifestyle, and she will never stop blaming him for losing that.

Let me point out something else to you: if Stephanie had made up a **No-No List,** she actually *could* have avoided this situation, not by listing "Embezzler," but by listing just two of her other big no-nos. What were they? As our discussion of their lifestyle went on, I discovered that it really bothered Stephanie that Mike had very little education. Due in part to a traumatic and impoverished childhood, he had never even earned a high school diploma. He would always have been hard-pressed to find a high-paying job. What's more, some of Mike's habits drove Stephanie up a wall, such as his poor English and uncultured table manners.

One of the things Stephanie nagged Mike about was the way he cut his meat. He could not help that. He had grown up with an abusive and drunken father and a mother who was rarely home because she was working hard to provide for the family. There had been nobody home to nurture him, much less teach him table manners. Such ingrained habits were not going to change.

It comes down to this: If you want to live with him, live with him. If you don't, *"Adios!"*

Two things should have been on Stephanie's **No-No List** from the start: "Uneducated," and "Unlikely to make a good living." Those no-nos should have meant *never-ever* to Stephanie. She could not belittle this guy into changing. He was trying as hard as he could, and her efforts to improve him only made him feel worse.

The problem with someone like Stephanie is that she could not admit she even had those no-nos on her list. It was easier to blame another person for failing to live up to his potential, rather than risk looking snobby or spoiled. If her **No-No List** had said from the start, "I do not want anybody who cannot provide a comfortable lifestyle," she probably could have found the right partner. She was middle class, educated, and pretty.

There is nothing wrong with wanting to be comfortable. There *is* something wrong with punishing someone because you cannot admit it.

Do you know why Stephanie picked Mike in the first place? "Because he loved me so much." For Mike, it was love at first sight. She was beautiful. For Stephanie, his romantic gestures sealed the deal. He swept her off her feet with roses, expensive dinners, and sweet words. When chemistry faded, they were left with problems they had failed to consider. If they had made **No-No Lists**, they might have spared themselves the agony their marriage became.

If Stephanie and Mike had made No-No Lists:

- Stephanie would have considered that an uneducated, uncultured man was unlikely to provide the luxurious life she wanted.
- Mike would have realized that Stephanie's desire for the easy life was likely to pose a lifetime challenge for him.

If they had made those lists, they might have married other people and lived happily ever after.

Let's Break This Down

How do you use a **No-No List** to avoid ending up like Stephanie and Mike, or countless other couples with dreamy beginnings and nightmare endings? Let's consider an imaginary woman who has just met a great guy. We will call the woman Jill and the man Jack. Jill finds Jack exciting, charming, smart, and good looking. Both Jill and Jack enjoy traveling, playing tennis, reading murder mysteries, listening to classic rock, and watching indie films. Both Jill and Jack are conservative, Catholic, and

Latino. Both Jill and Jack are casual people whose top values are loyalty, family, and service to their fellow humans. Sounds like a match made in heaven, right? Not necessarily. We are still only talking about 31 percent of their relationship.

The important thing is to find out what is going on in the 69 percent of the relationship that they do not have in common. That is where the no-nos always are. So Jill is going to look for no-nos, and hope there aren't too many. When Jill has some time alone she checks her **No-No List**. She pulls out Worksheet #2, and sees that her list of ten traits to avoid includes the following five: "Dependent," "Procrastinator," "Compulsive," "Perfection-ist," "Antisocial." Then she starts writing about her new prospect in the blanks. Despite the heart-thumping chemistry, she recalls red flags that indicate Jack has hit four of the five above items.

Here are some of the clues that Jack is not right for Jill:

Jack keeps asking his friends' opinions on what to order at restaurants, his last girlfriend picked his clothes, and he lives with his parents. Those are red flags for: "Dependent." While Jack and Jill are at a party, Jack tells her about multiple deadlines he has missed at work: "Procrastinator." Jack refuses to go to a movie unless everyone arrives a half-hour early because he fears he will miss the previews, and he will not let his dog back in the house until it goes number two, even when it is snowing: "Com-pulsive." Jack runs the Dustbuster every time someone spills the tiniest crumb at his house, stacks all his work papers perfectly, and corrects everyone's grammar: "Perfectionist." Maybe Jack is gregarious, so at least he is not antisocial, but he has a lot of no-nos going for him.

In this scenario, I would not recommend that Jill date Jack, despite all they have in common.

It is possible some of the above red flags are isolated inci-dents, but I doubt it. There is a reason those traits ended up on

Jill's **No-No List**. Jill is probably all too familiar with people who have those quirks, and dating them has not gone well in the past. Jill knows the signs. So, even though 31 percent of the potential relationship sounds awesome, the problem is that these problems fall within the 69 percent that covers more than twice the territory of any relationship. This is especially important when we consider that we have not even talked about Jill's 69 percent, which Jack might not like so much either.

A solid marriage is not as much about common interests as it is about common values. I will admit it is not always easy to know how to evaluate that. Everyone believes his values are good, so if we meet someone we like and that person is decent, it is easy to assume his or her values are fine. They might be fine, but they might not be yours. The **No-No List** helps you identify these differences more clearly, by drawing strong boundaries that cannot be crossed.

If you feel strongly about your religious or political beliefs, then someone from a different party or religion is probably a Never-Ever, even if that person reveals no other No-No.

When it comes to core values, differences in religion or politics are the death knell for marital harmony. Sure, a few people make bi-political or bi-religious marriages work, but they are too few and far between to take such a risk on someone you have not started dating yet. Nip that one in the bud before you buy yourself a world of trouble. Actually, I would be surprised if such a person did not hit several other no-nos on your list anyway, because your spiritual and political beliefs form the foundation for many of your other attitudes and behaviors. As far as I'm concerned, sharply divergent religious or political beliefs are never-evers.

The great thing about the **No-No List** is that it gets you out of the realm of thinking philosophically about values and gives you a more concrete way to measure and interpret those values. Articulating what we value, even for educated people who live the examined life, is a difficult thing to do with certainty. The **No-No List** adds a bit more assurance to the mix.

Opposites Attract, but Not for Long

Opposites do attract, but do they make good marriages? It depends which aspects of your lives we are talking about. Are you just different from each other, or diametrically opposed?

Let's say you are an organized, responsible person. It makes sense that you might be attracted to someone relaxed and casual, someone who exhibits a side of yourself that you have never developed and might like to explore. It can be fun to spend time with this uncontrolled person who makes you feel like you can let your hair down. But if this other person wants to move from place to place when you prefer to be grounded, or drops projects to go out and play when commitment is critical to you, or just seems plain irresponsible: run for your life! Because you are so responsible, that childlike irresponsibility will ultimately instigate terrible arguments. The very thing you loved about the other person could become the thing you hate.

Opposites might attract in the short run, but they are unlikely to last long unless each accepts the other for who they are. You have to ask yourself: is this just a fun surface difference that acts as a great balance to an undeveloped side of you, or is this a difference that reflects something in your core values that you only fantasize changing but are unlikely to compromise long term? If the answer is the latter, I suggest you stop the relationship before it even starts.

To put it more simply: if I love chocolate and he loves vanilla, no problem. Maybe this week we buy vanilla ice cream and next week we buy chocolate. Or maybe I don't mind eating vanilla for the rest of my life. But if he is a glutton and a couch potato who eats a pint of vanilla ice cream in one sitting, and I am a health nut who is turned off by people who don't take care of themselves, we might have a long-term conflict brewing.

If you cannot live with it, know this:
You will not be able to change it.

If you cannot live with something because it goes against your beliefs, and you meet someone who does it all the time, then that **No-No** is a **Never-Ever**. Shake that person's hand, say, "It was nice meeting you," and keep your eyes peeled for the next opportunity. Someone who shares your values is out there, but if you waste your time with Mr. or Ms. Never-Ever, you might miss your chance.

Chapter 12

X X X ✔

Deciding to Live with a No-No

How Important Is It?

So you find a man or woman who shows a lot of potential in the relationship department, but when you do your homework you find out that this person definitely has a few traits that are on your **No-No List**. It is time for the big question: how important is it?

Is this a big problem or a small one? Does she complain *a lot*, or only in rare situations? Does he yell a lot, or only on the freeway? Can you ignore the no-no because everything else about this person is amazing? Maybe you will learn to appreciate that this apparent flaw has its advantages: maybe her willingness to complain goes hand-in-hand with a knack for solving problems, maybe he only lets loose his aggressive side to protect people he cares about.

Sometimes what looks like a
No-No is really a *Maybe*.

Character traits rarely reveal themselves in black and white. Most people never switch their bad behaviors 100 percent on or off. Humans are nuanced. That is why the worksheets I have provided give you an opportunity to rate no-nos on a scale of 1 to 10, 1 being only a minor annoyance, and 10 being something you would only tolerate with a gun to your head.

Even if you find someone who seems perfect in every way, you will likely find that you can still check off at least a couple of items on your **No-No List**. That is when you need to pause and ask yourself, "Is this going to be a problem or not?" Are you looking at two tiny red flags, neither of which rises to a 5 rating? That is probably not a problem. Are you looking at four red flags, all of them at or below a 5 rating? That might be a problem, or it might not. Are you looking at only two red flags, but both scream for a rating of 10? It seems likely to me that those will be a problem. Still, the decision is up to you.

Relationships require negotiation, not only between you and another person, but also within yourself.

Let us once again think of this in terms of Jill and Jack with Jill evaluating Jack for no-nos. Maybe Jack has some negative traits Jill does not want, such as being *compulsive* and *dependent*, but maybe those traits show up in a subtle way. Let's take these one at a time, starting with *compulsive*. Maybe Jack's red flags are that he does not like it when his foods touch each other on the plate, that he alphabetizes his DVDs, and that he always wears a red tie on Mondays. Sure, those things are a little compulsive, but if it does not go much beyond that then maybe this is a quirk Jill can live with.

Now let's consider Jack's red flags when it comes to the no-no of being "Dependent." Maybe Jack prefers a little encouragement before making a decision: "I think I want to enter the contest, but I'm not sure this is my best work. What do you think, friends?" That might indicate a bit of insecurity, but more likely it simply reveals someone who values the opinion of trusted friends. Either way, it probably does not indicate deep dependency.

You will never find anybody who does not exhibit at least one trait from your No-No List. Nobody is that perfect.

If someone only lightly taps a couple of no-nos on your list, then the 69 percent of the relationship that you do not share in common may not pose a major problem. In fact, such a person is probably worth the trouble, considering that anyone you choose will always differ from you in about 69 percent of the relationship, and that 69 percent will always present a few no-nos. Ultimately it comes down to you being protective about the no-nos that most reflect a departure from your values. You need to work at differentiating between the potential date who exhibits your no-nos with vigor and the one who only has a couple of minor quirks.

Experience Teaches Us What to Let Go

If you have been in a lot of relationships that failed, you might fear that relationships are always more trouble than they are worth. That is just not so. In fact, you truly can turn negative experiences to positive advantage. If you are past the age of sixteen, then experience has probably thrown you at least a few relationship issues you have promised yourself you will never live with again: "I do not want somebody who does this," or "I am not going to change myself to accommodate that." If you go through a lot of relationships that do not work out, each succeeding time it can feel increasingly difficult to make the leap of faith. But each succeeding time you have more information to help you make a better choice. You just need a tool to put what you have learned to effective use. That tool is the **No-No List.**

The modern trend toward acceptance of divorce, living together, and premarital sex makes it easier to get out of nightmare relationships. In many situations, that can be a lifesaver. However, if you are not careful, it can also make it easier to leap before you look, knowing you have a safety net. It can make it too easy to follow only your heart and forget your head, knowing you can escape if your heart is wrong. If you end up in a lot of short-term, unworkable relationships, society might not shun you, but you might find yourself shying away from commitment.

Each time your past relationships failed, your list of no-nos grew. That is not all bad news. A No-No List can put all your bad experiences from past failures to work for you.

Relationships that work require work, and if we are smart we will put that effort in from the start. The rewards are waiting, if you do your homework. That means thinking carefully about your **No-No List.** You need to think through what you *truly* don't want, not what you think you are *supposed* to reject. That is one way to avoid repeating past mistakes. The other way is to figure out how much you are willing to sacrifice to have the relationship you say you want. If you want the joy of connection with another human being, you will always have to pay some sort of price. Nothing worthwhile is easy. You must be willing to completely accept this person's behavior, values, and interests, not just put up with them.

"Putting up with it" is an attitude that implies judgment and resentment. It is a way of saying that you do not entirely accept this person as he or she is, that you will only love some parts of this person and reserve the right to hold the rest against him or her at a later date. That is just no way to love other people. It is bad for them and it is bad for you. You will both end up suffering.

You need to be willing to either ignore without judgment, or embrace wholeheartedly, even those parts of this person that do not represent your own values, interests, or understanding. All the better if you are willing to take it a step further and support your partner in independent pursuits that do not involve you, pursuits that allow this person to grow in directions that might not be important to you but are important to him or her.

It helps to remember that your willingness to support your partner even in those areas that do not interest you or that you do not understand will engender gratitude in the right partner. That gratitude will make a good partner all the more willing to support you in your own independent pursuits.

You might ultimately discover that some of those differences you have decided to live with are not only not as negative as you thought, but also have their benefits. Sometimes it is in our differences that we gain the most in relationships. Each of us brings something unique to the relationship that strengthens, supports, and enhances what our partner has to offer. We may discover new interests, or simply learn gratitude for someone who accepts us with all our quirks and foibles, someone who is not threatened by our strengths or outside interests. Deciding to live with a no-no here and there can help us grow as people. If you find someone with whom you are willing to do that with open eyes and an open heart, it will be worth your while.

The key to a successful relationship is to support your partner in expressing the best of himself or herself, even if doing so sometimes takes that person in a different direction from you. That is part of what it means to take each other for better or worse. Sometimes we need to stop using the word "worse," and just let it be.

If you have had trouble "letting it be" in the past, had trouble supporting the parts of another person that you did not understand, that may be because you chose a partner who was inappropriate for you. However, when you find a partner who is appropriate, you may well discover that this person too needs your support in areas of his or her life that you do not understand. This need for support, even in the separate parts of our lives, is something everyone has. When you encounter it, you need not fear that this relationship will fail like the others. Rather, this may be your opportunity to get it right. With the use of your **No-No List** you will not be blindsided, because you have identified this need beforehand and accepted it as something you can and will deal with. With the right person, you will find it in yourself to let it be.

You may discover that your previous partners' inability to relate to some of your unique ways is not peculiar to them. You will always have some need or want that a partner will not understand, even when you find the right person. With the **No-No List**, you will discover these issues with eyes open. That improves your chance to find someone who will accept and support the things that make you different, making you happier to do the same for that person in return.

What We Gain from Acceptance

People joke that marriage is an institution in more ways than one. People who are happily married laugh affectionately at the idea, knowing that they share a sort of mutually accepted madness with their loved one: "He is a little eccentric about this, and I am a little quirky about that, and we would not change anything about each other." People who are stuck in unhappy marriages laugh more stridently at the idea of being locked up in an "institution": "It's worse!" they might say. "I'd rather be in a padded cell than put up with her insane behavior one more minute!" On the other hand, sometimes the very same quality one spouse considers a curse in a partner, another considers a blessing: "My husband is so detail-oriented it drives me crazy!" versus, "Really? Mine is so detail-oriented it makes me wild!"

I have a male friend who got married, who had no professional ambitions. He decided he was going to be a stay-at-home dad. His wife was thrilled with the arrangement. She was an ambitious doctor, but she wanted a family and felt it was important that somebody stay home with the kids. They have enjoyed a long and happy marriage. When the kids went off to college, the father studied to become a chef, a respectable dream to follow, but perhaps not everyone's stereotypical image of ambitious masculinity. His wife recently told me, "Everyone makes fun of me." That's because they see it as a role reversal. Nonetheless, she does not let the teasing bother her, because the relationship works. "He sacrificed a lot for our kids, so if now he wants to pursue his dream to become a chef, that's fine with me."

Other women might prefer more ambition in a mate. They might prefer that both husband and wife work outside the home to contribute to the financial pool. Some ambitious women, and men for that matter, do not want to feel alone in financially supporting the family. For such women, my friend's situation would have been a no-no. By the same token, their situations would likely have been a no-no for her, because she would have had to either give up some of her goals to take on more home-front responsibilities or worry about shortchanging her kids.

Another woman I know discovered that her husband was cheating on her. Instead of confronting him, she decided not to mention it. She admitted that cheating was a no-no in her book, but she was too invested in other aspects of the relationship to rock the boat. She said, more or less, "I don't want him to cheat, but if he knows that I know, then he won't even try to hide it anymore and we won't have any peace in the house. I might decide on a divorce later, but for now I'm going to make the sacrifice because he's a fantastic father."

Her children were in their early teens when she discovered his infidelity, and she had just gone back to work. She decided that she would use the next few years to build her career, and then when the kids went to college and did not have as great a need for parenting, she would divorce him. Until then, she would just keep greeting him with a smile when he came home. For her, the benefits of being married to a fantastic father, who was an otherwise reasonable housemate, were worth the trade-off of living with a man who cheated.

That story makes no sense to me as a wife and mother, but makes perfect sense to me as a therapist. In her shoes, I would have been enraged by his disrespect and dishonesty. To me, getting away from him would be the best way to protect myself and my children. She took a different view. She did not want her children to face the disruption of separate homes, parents at odds, and reduced financial status. She wanted them to have private schools, a secure household, and parents who got along. She determined what she valued most in the relationship and the price she was willing to pay for it. She made a conscious choice. Nothing wrong with that.

> Finding the right person does not always mean avoiding No-Nos. It means learning to evaluate them in the context of real situations.

Other no-nos yield more easily to compromise. I love to travel and have adventures, but my husband prefers to enjoy peace and quiet at home. This would fit him under one of my no-no categories: "Boring." For many years we pushed and pulled at each other on this subject: "Where's your sense of adventure?" versus "Why do you try to make me go places where I won't be comfortable?" When we did travel, I wanted to wake early to sightsee, while he wanted to sleep in and hang out by the pool. My logic was, "Why just sit around? We can do that at home." His logic was, "Why run around exhausting ourselves? We might as well be at work."

I even love trips where things go wrong because that is where the adventure is. Here is the catch: I do not like that sort of experience in daily life. When I am working or relaxing at home, I want predictability. My husband is great at keeping things on an even keel. So, this no-no only affected a small part of our lives. I was not about to give up my marriage over it.

We came up with a solution. I have fun traveling with my sister, who has a sense of adventure. She is open to new experiences, does not like a set itinerary, and loves last-minute plans. My sister's concept of packing is to take everything out of the laundry basket, dump it into her suitcase, and zip it. Throughout the entire trip, she is always missing things: "Venus, did you bring this? Venus, can I borrow that?" I am organized, so I always have what I need. In daily life, my sister's disorganized streak would drive me mad, but that is fine because I do not live with her. While traveling, we have hilarious adventures, meet unusual people, and see things we did not expect. So I satisfy my travel bug, and I am grateful to come home to my "dull" but dependable spouse. He is happy to be off the hook as my travel partner.

My husband and I do still travel together, sometimes with our son and the rest of the family. Those trips are tamer, but that is fine with me because at least we are on the road with the family, and I know I will feed my need for adventure with my sister on another trip.

Sometimes **No-Nos** become *Maybes* with the help of basic compromise.

No one partner will ever fill all your needs. Maybe you can get some needs met another way. In turn, maybe you can let your partner meet a few needs without you. The question is simple: how important is it that you and your partner be in tandem for this aspect of your life together? The answer is not always easy. The important thing is to have conversations about your hot buttons, both with yourself and with the other person, before the relationship even begins.

One Person's No-No is Another's Treasure

When people feel bad about themselves in relationships, it is often because their partners try to change them or because they feel the need to change for their partner. Those are *never-evers* in any relationship, even if society agrees that it is reasonable to want to change that no-no. Maybe society considers it reasonable to expect a partner to pick clothes up off the floor. Then again, maybe society sees it the other way: that it is reasonable to leave clothes lying around if you are busy. It all becomes personal perspective. What is reasonable is up to the two of you, but picking the partner with whom you can decide those things is at first up to just one person: you.

A romance or marriage is not between you and society's expectations. It is between you and one person.

When you consider potential people to date, remember your list is only a guide. People are not lists. The **No-No List** is not going to make your decision for you. It is only going to focus your attention on the critical question you need to ask yourself: can I live with this person?

One couple I know always has to discuss every little purchase they make. Even if she wants to go to Wal-Mart to buy dishes, she has to ask her husband. If my husband expected that from me it would be a no-no in my book. I do not even have to check with him if I want to buy a couch. When I do mention such plans, he says, "Honey, that is your department." By contrast, my friend's husband wants her to account for every little fifty-dollar expense before she spends it. If my husband expected that, I would be angry at him for treating me like a child.

My friend does not see it that way. She likes that her husband sets a budget for her and that he makes the final decision. To her way of thinking, this gives her more freedom rather than less, because it frees her from having to deliberate over choices. These are the parameters, she stays within them, and the mystery is taken out of the process. He worries about the money, and all she has to do is spend it according to pre-set standards. To her that is easier. You might think she is a homemaker, but no, she has a career. Her salary goes into their joint account, but he is the one who makes spending decisions. She does not even question him. I would be shouting, "This money is as much mine as yours!" To her it is not sexist, just practical. For her, it works.

Most people would prefer not to have a relationship with someone they consider domineering or controlling, so you might think you must include those items on your **No-No List**. Don't be so sure. You might discover that you like the idea of someone else taking on responsibilities that you find daunting or dull. Just be careful. When you give up control in one part of your life, it can be all too easy to give it up in another. It is best to begin thinking early about the larger implications that one small no-no might have down the line. Is the other person controlling the money just to take weight off your shoulders, or might this individual want to control everything about you? Could it start with planning the budget and end with planning your career? If you wait until you are in a relationship to think about these things, it could be too late.

Make sure you know what you are saying "No" to.

One person's **No-No** is another person's **Yes-Yes**. Do not feel as if you have to fill your **No-No List** with those things you believe you are *supposed* to hate. Make sure you list only the things that you truly do not like. This is not about "shoulds" or "should nots;" it is about you and what you truly do and don't want. Remember, those things you *don't* want are where the problems will come from, so make sure you really understand what they are.

"Putting Up With" No-Nos Kills Relationships

Many marriages only survive because the husbands and wives avoid each other. Many such people keep living together only because they find it more convenient than going through a messy divorce. Such relationships are filled with resentment. Who walks into a relationship hoping to end up like that? Nobody. I still love spending time with my husband, even though he is very different from me. You can find a relationship like that too, if you remember one critical thing: you cannot just marry part of a person, you have to marry the whole package.

Accepting someone is not just a matter
of putting up with things you hate.

The attitude of "putting up with someone" is a relationship No-No.

If you find a no-no in someone and tell yourself, "I'll put up with it," or "I'll deal with it since this person has to deal with me," that is not going to work. If you get into a relationship with the faintest hope that this no-no might go away, that you might train your partner out of it, or that you can use it as leverage to get your way later—"Hey, I put up with this thing I hate, so you have to let me do that thing you hate"—that will not work either. Doing any of those things is going to land you in a relationship full of resentment.

Part of what keeps my relationship with my spouse lively is that we do not merely put up with each other's differences. We embrace them. This allows us to dive into lively conversations about the parts of our lives that do *not* intersect. There is still plenty of time that we spend apart, each of us pursuing our own interests and needs, and because we are okay with that, there is not only a lack of recrimination over our separate activities, there is also plenty to talk about. We pick at each other's brains and revel in discovering how different we are, what unique things we bring to the table, what ideas we never thought of before. Many of those no-nos we have come to embrace in each other will give us plenty to talk about for the rest of our lives.

True Love Requires Sacrifice

When you begin a new relationship, you can no longer think only about what you want. You must find a way to mesh what you want with what someone else wants. No matter how good you are at using your **No-No List** to weed out wrong prospects, you are never going to end up in a relationship in which you and your partner always want the same thing. So, if you want a lasting relationship, you will have to make concessions. Period.

Also, remember it is possible to be dating for months or to be married for years and suddenly be confronted with no-nos that never came up before. That is why it is so important to minimize the number of no-nos you have to deal with from the start.

Whatever you do not like about your partner now, at best it will probably stay the same over time. More likely, it will get worse. So decide now: can you keep making the sacrifice?

Books are one of my passions, and marrying a man who was well read was important to me. An uneducated man would have been a no-no. At the beginning of our relationship, I continued with my passion for reading. After the birth of my son, my reading was reduced to reading in the bathroom or at bedtime. I had to give up a little ground on that passion of mine, not because my husband failed to support my love for books, but because we had a child who needed feeding, changing, and driving to school, who needed discipline, help with homework, and nurturing in his interests. My reading took second place. I had to make a sacrifice.

On the other hand, my husband and child also made sacrifices for me. For example, sometimes I would go into the bathroom, lock the door, and insist on my time to read. Nobody was allowed to interrupt me during my me-time.

Family has meant sacrifices for all of us, but it has been a modern sacrifice: we have each sacrificed something for the whole, but the whole has also sacrificed so we can meet our individual needs. Sacrifice has its gifts.

> Mutual sacrifice can be mutually beneficial, but many people fail to do it because the sacrifice always seems bigger when you are the one making it.

On your **No-No List**, you give your no-nos numerical values, but when you make sacrifices, those sacrifices cannot be measured. They are a matter of empathy and love-in-action. You might worry that your partner will spend so much time at dance classes or in front of the TV that it will take away from time with you. But do not be in a rush to list such things as no-nos. Remember that there are also things you will want to do that are just for you and nobody else, and at some point your partner will have to sacrifice so that you can do them.

Whatever your no-nos are, flexibility must always play a role. It is inevitable in any relationship that someday you will have to make sacrifices. The question is: Have you found enough of value in the person before you, have you eliminated enough of the **No-Nos**, to make it clear to you that this is someone for whom you will make those sacrifices gladly?

Appendix A

Steps to Making & Using Your No-No List

1. Use the sample Worksheet #1 to create your No-No List.
2. Choose about 10 No-Nos that you are certain you don't want in a potential partner. Use the suggestions on Worksheet #1 or add your own No-Nos.
3. Define your No-Nos and find out what they mean to you. I suggest going even deeper to find out why these traits are so important to you and why they trigger you. This step is very important. Due diligence in this step will help you to get to know yourself at a deeper level.
4. Use a rating scale of 1 to 10 to rank how important it is to you to avoid someone with each listed trait. A number 1 indicates less importance, while a 10 indicates critical importance. You do not need to assign each trait a different number. In other words, you can have several items listed as 3s, or 7s, or 10s.
5. Transfer your 10 or so No-Nos to Worksheet #2, ordering them from the highest number rank to the lowest.
6. Make multiple copies of your filled-out Worksheet #2, and use one for each potential date.
7. Observe the potential date/mate in a natural setting. Focus on the specific words, attitudes, habits, and behaviors of the prospect in question. This will help you identify how this person measures up against your No-Nos. This person

might even present a couple of potential No-Nos that you forgot to include in your original list or that you have never before considered. Revise your list as needed.

8. After each meeting you have with the prospect, continue to revise your Worksheet #2.

   a. Mark only those negative traits from your **No-No List** that you suspect the prospect might have.

   b. Describe the red flags that indicate he or she might have those traits.

   c. Rank how strongly the prospect appears to exhibit each No-No trait on a scale of one to ten.

9. After a few observations, if the prospect exhibits two or more traits that you have rated five or higher in your "Value to you" column, and if he or she exhibits those traits at a ranking of five or higher, then I would not suggest going on a first date.

10. For anything that falls below the lines I've described in #9, I suggest you study your list and decide how important those things are to you in the long term.

Rating each No-No on a scale of 1-10 gives you a mathematical way to weigh the pros and cons of a potential relationship. However, you still have to subjectively decide if the way a particular person exhibits a no-no makes it a deal breaker, a potential problem or challenge, or nothing more than a minor annoyance. How much does it take to tip the scales against deciding to date this person: five small no-nos? one huge one? three medium-sized ones? The bottom line is: Can you live with it? You have to ask yourself: "If this behavior never changed, could I live with it?" If not, you should give a thumbs-down to even going on a first date.

If you believe that the person you are interested in has enough going for him or her that you could graciously surrender an item or two on your list, then go on the first date. If you decide to date this person, know that these traits will not change. You need to accept them as is.

Appendix B

Worksheets

WORKSHEET #1

No-Nos (Non-Negotiables)	Red Flags/Definitions	Your own definitions	Value to you 1 - 10
Boring	Quiet, does not initiate anything, likes status quo		
Cold mannered	Detached, aloof, disengaged		
Stingy	Does not tip adequately, goes to extremes to save a buck		
Not intellectually stimulating	Does not appreciate challenging books, movies, TV shows, or news programs		
Dependent	Waits for others to decide everything, won't voice likes or dislikes, always relies on others		
Suffocating/ Needy	Wants to always be with you, does not allow room for personal growth, needs constant attention		
Controlling	Wants to tell people what to do all the time, thinks he/she is always right, wants to change everything about you		
Haunted by the past	Lives in the past, cannot get excited about the present or future, makes no room for a new relationship		
Holds a grudge	Remembers the past and won't let it go, not forgiving		

No-Nos (Non-Negotiables)	Red Flags/Definitions	Your own definitions	Value to you 1 - 10
Dishonest	Takes pride in fooling other people, lies about age to get discounts, cheats the IRS		
Irresponsible	Does not pay bills on time, does not show up to work on time, does not finish projects, does not keep promises		
Never owns up to mistakes/ Blamer	Never admits being wrong, often blames others for his/her own mistakes, always has an excuse, problems are always somebody else's fault (i.e. in previous relationships)		
Depressed	Downer, pessimistic, always talking about the dark side of things		
Shrewd/ Cunning	Does not stop at any-thing to get what he/she wants		
Egotistic/ Selfish	It is all about him/her, has to get what he/she wants, ignores the needs of others		
Manipulative	Treats other people as pawns in a game meant to benefit him/her, always seeks to turn other people's interests or problems to his/her advantage, uses people		

(continued)

No-Nos (Non-Negotiables)	Red Flags/Definitions	Your own definitions	Value to you 1 - 10
Know-it-all	Never wrong, knows what's best for everybody, grandiose talk or behavior		
Argumentative	Every conversation turns into an argument until you agree with the person		
Temperamental	Constantly screams at or harasses other drivers in traffic, throws a fit in restaurants or stores when service people make mistakes, loses temper whenever things don't go his/her way		
Workaholic	Walks, talks, and breathes nothing but work, does not have a balanced life		
Addiction	Abuses or engages to excess in drugs, alcohol, cigarettes, food, sex, shopping, gambling, etc.; has a generally addictive personality		
Unmotivated	Needs a force behind him/her to get anything done, needs constant coaxing or convincing to pursue goals		
Couch potato	Does not like active life, watches TV more often than any other leisure activity, may also be an introvert		

No-Nos (Non-Negotiables)	Red Flags/Definitions	Your own definitions	Value to you 1 - 10
Promiscuous	Makes constant sexual, suggestive, or appraising comments about the opposite sex; brags about previous sexual relationships; does not take commitments seriously; cheats		
Looking for short-term relationship	Long list of previous relationships, lack of commitment		
Lacks loyalty	Talks negatively about family, employer, or friends when they're not present to defend themselves; lack of gratitude		
Competitive	Does anything to win in sports, talks about coworkers as if they're enemies, vies for attention, always needs to get the credit, can't work well in a group		
Perfectionist	Everything has to be organized, cannot stand departing from routine, nothing is ever good enough, never satisfied with self, never quits trying to improve self and world		
Victim mentality	Behaves or speaks as if the world is out to get him/her, "poor me" attitude		

(continued)

No-Nos (Non-Negotiables)	Red Flags/Definitions	Your own definitions	Value to you 1 - 10
Sexist	Expresses that women/men are only good at certain things, expresses that women/men are incapable of certain things, complains when the opposite sex does something that falls outside gender norms or stereotypes (i.e. men should be handy around the house, men should not cry, women should cook, women should not be in charge)		
Violent	Should be on everybody's list		
Religion mismatch			
Social class mismatch			
Cultural mismatch			
Lack of financial security/ wealth			

WORKSHEET #2

No-Nos (Non-Negotiables)	Your own definitions	Value to you 1 - 10	Exhibited red flags	Prospect ranking 1 - 10

About the Author

Venus Rouhani came into marriage counseling in an unusual way: She began her career in dentistry—both as a practitioner and in academia. During that time, she earned a reputation for her ability to calm patients' fear of dental work. After she suffered a shoulder injury, her work as a dentist came to an end, and a career in therapy was the natural next step. Venus earned a master's degree in counseling and is dual licensed in marriage and family therapy and professional counseling,

In her thriving therapy practice in Austin, Texas, Venus regularly sees struggling couples and individuals frustrated in their search for a lasting and happy romantic partnership. Through working with her clients, she has discovered that identifying clearly what you don't want in a mate is the crucial first step in knowing yourself and finding the right partner. The principles she shares in *The No-No List* are built around this premise. Venus also attributes much of the success of her marriage of over forty years to these principles.

www.ingramcontent.com/pod-product-compliance
Lightning Source LLC
Chambersburg PA
CBHW031844090426
42741CB00005B/345